When you love a child

◊

*For the times
when caring for kids
is difficult*

Harriet Hodgson

Deaconess Press

This book is dedicated to my daughters. I love you and am fiercely proud of you both.

First Published March, 1992.
©1992 by Harriet Hodgson. All rights reserved.
Printed in the United States of America.

96 95 94 93 92   5 4 3 2 1

Cover design by Kathy Boardman, Minneapolis, MN
Illustration by Patrick Faricy, Minneapolis, MN

ISBN: 0-925190-51-9
Library of Congress Catalog Card Number 91-077592

Preface

During these fast-paced times, many of us are turning to self-help books for comfort, only to discover that comfort comes from within. Meditation helps us to define our parenting roles and, indeed, ourselves.

This book follows the standard meditation format. Each day begins with a short quotation, followed by a meditation which amplifies the quote and concludes with a summary. Because it is easier to remember a single point, rather than many, I have written one-sentence summaries, or "thought bullets."

Take a few moments to flip through the book and scan the summaries. Notice the parallel sentence structure. The word "will", symbolic of the dedication of loving parents, is always followed by an action verb—words like try, share, seek, plan, cope, give and love. Every summary is an affirmation of parenting.

You don't have to read the meditations in order. Match the meditation to your day. Some days you may only have enough time to read the summary. Re-read the meditations that have special meaning to you. Use the space at the bottom of the page to jot down your thoughts.

This journal space can help you to identify feelings, figure out what's important, see where you have come from and make you aware of where you are headed. Complete sentences aren't necessary. Record key words, or phrases, even drawings—anything that will jog your memory later.

The meditations cover the full scope of parenting: infancy, toddler years, elementary years, adolescence, adult children and grandchildren. Finding a year's worth of quotes proved to be a research challenge. The quotes I selected—everything from Confucius to Cosby—are a sampling from many different corners of literature.

As people learned I was writing this book, they invariably asked, "Where did you find the quotes?" I was asked the question again and again. Curiosity was so great that I decided to include my reference list in the book. Some listings are passing asides, but others are worth further exploration.

Each of us brings a unique family history to parenting. However, we don't have to repeat this history. We can discard emotional baggage, clarify values, identify choices, explore creative ideas, weigh options, take chances and craft new parenting patterns. That's what I did.

Since I was a child, I've been crazy about kids. Somehow I thought this love, coupled with two college degrees in education, were preventive medicine. I thought I would be an exception, a blip on the parenting chart, and wouldn't make the same mistakes my parents made.

You know what happened. I made many of the mistakes my parents made and more. My children weren't perfect, nor was I the perfect parent. As the decades passed, however, I was able to see parenting more clearly. I understood the lifetime commitment parenting involved. Today I parent my adult daughters from afar in new and ever-changing ways.

All of the meditations are indexed by subject for quick reference. The meditations are not replacements for thought, they are precursors to thought, a bridge between your daily life and your inner journey. Nobody can tell you how to parent your children. You will discover that for yourself and in your own time.

Harriet Hodgson

January 1

LOVE/CHANGE

The new year begins . . . a new resolve . . . to show the love—to live it.

Governor Mario Cuomo

◊

Having a baby has changed us forever. Life seems richer, filled with the child's surprises of physical growth, signs of personality and speech development. It seems as if our baby changes from hour to hour.

We cheer when cooing turns into syllables, syllables turn into words, and words turn into sentences. And we are surprised at how much companionship a baby provides. But it is not the baby that has changed us, it is love.

All the love we had locked inside us has come out. This love not only illuminates our lives, it illuminates the lives of all we meet. Love was meant to be shared.

◊

I will show love for my children.

_____

_____

_____

_____

_____

January 2

PATIENCE

It's up to us to give our relationships a chance.
                                    Leo F. Buscaglia, Ph.D.

◊

How impatient we are! Like instant soup, we want instant parent-child relationships. The relationships between parents and children don't work that way.

Like seeds beneath the snow, parent–child relationships germinate and grow and bud into full flower. When these relationships falter, due to misunderstandings, truancy, delinquency, addiction, or other reasons, our patience is challenged. It is up to us to give our children—and ourselves—a chance.

Our children love us. If we are patient, love will bring them back to us again.

◊

I will be patient with my child and myself.

_____

_____

_____

_____

_____

January 3

ROLE MODELS

There was a child that went forth every day: and the first object he look'd upon, that object he became.

Walt Whitman

◊

Parents are some of the "objects" children see. Even before our baby is born, we begin to think about the role models we will become. Thinking about the task is challenging enough, without living it day after day.

We may forget about role models and concentrate on daily survival. In the middle of the night, when we cannot sleep, we grade ourselves on parenting. Perhaps we give ourselves an "A" for settling a squabble. Or we may give ourselves a "B" for soothing words. We are doing the best we can and hope it is enough.

The people we are determines, in part, the people our children will become.

◊

I will think about the role model I present.

January 4

IMMEDIACY

You have to give it (parenting) all you have, especially since you never know how long the good times will last.

Lee Iacocca

◊

We get caught up in our children's schedules: car pools, music lessons, homework, baseball games, school plays, scouts and more. The hurriedness of our lives causes us to lose perspective. Soon our children's schedules, and staying on schedule, are top priority.

Childhood schedules cannot be allowed to interfere with the joy of parenting. We need to mentally separate our children's schedules from children. Listening is one way to do this. The daily chatter helps us to piece together portraits of our children. These portraits remind us that the days of childhood are fleeting.

◊

I will savor the tiny moments of childhood.

_____

_____

_____

_____

_____

January 5

IMPERFECTION

Mothers are just normal people really.

                                        Erma Bombeck
◊

Sometimes we're so hard on ourselves. We think we have to be perfect parents. We vow not to make the same mistakes our parents made. After all, things have changed in the information age. But we need to ask ourselves one question: Did a perfect parent ever exist?

The fact is, children learn from our imperfection. They see us as ordinary people who fail and then have the courage to try again. When our children become parents they will know, from life experience, that parents come in different sizes, shapes, colors, talents, temperaments, and flaws. Without guarantees.
◊

I will discard thoughts of perfection and enjoy this imperfect day.

_____

_____

_____

_____

_____

January 6

HERITAGE

My son and I are both tall fellows...

Garrison Keillor

◊

We have all heard about genetic influences, but seeing them in real life is boggling, if not amazing. Our children's physical resemblances to grandparents make us think of the past and dream of the future.

In addition to signs of our children's physical heritage, we see signs of their emotional heritage as well. We joke about Irish tempers and Scandinavian stubbornness and German precision. Our jokes are evidence of the wonder of genetic imprinting.

◊

I will find joy in my children's heritage.

_____

_____

_____

_____

_____

January 7

CHILDCARE/WONDER

After you've made your rounds you fall asleep in the center, watched over by your bear, your camel, your mobile. Watched over by me.

                                                                Phyllis Chesler

◊

A sleeping child is peaceful, yet cries out to us in beauty. Looking at our child, fanny in the air, clutching a quilt, hugging a frayed teddy bear, makes us smile. Is this the same child who was wildly running around a few minutes ago?

We stagger to bed. As we drift off to sleep, we replay snatches of the day's conversations. "I want a birthday cake with purple roses...That hamster is always running away...I love you Mommy...You're the best–est Daddy."

And we think of how rewarding parenting can be. Even as we sleep, we are attuned to the needs of our children.

◊

I will look upon my sleeping child and cherish the moment.

_____

_____

_____

_____

_____

January 8

IDENTITY/HERITAGE

I started the process of learning to treat my daughter as a separate person with an identity of her own.

Margaret Mead

◊

Because we are our children's birth parents, we may treat them as extensions of ourselves. When we do this we are forgetting the miracle of genetics. There are no two children in the world that are identical, not even identical twins.

This mathematical miracle is almost beyond understanding. We see our children as separate individuals, with identities of their own. Our children's uniqueness will help them to find their paths in life. As mature parents, we will encourage them to do just that.

◊

I will encourage my children's uniqueness.

_____

_____

_____

_____

_____

January 9

DREAMS

Anything can happen, child, ANYTHING can be.
                                                            Shel Silverstein

◊

The dreams of childhood are many things: silly, scary, redundant, hilarious, and serious. As children divulge their dreams to us, we become frightened for them. We see the future through adult eyes, focusing on education, impending conflict, even failure.

We must be careful not to project our fears upon our children. Letting children have their dreams is part of letting go. Therefore, we will encourage our children's dreams. For without dreams, what is life?

◊

I will listen attentively to my child's dreams.

_____

_____

_____

_____

_____

January 10

EMPTY-NEST

No more children would be living at home. The readjustments to being alone...with no children about, would be difficult.

Eleanor Roosevelt

◊

After the children are gone we think our parenting days are over. No children's voices are heard in the house, no muddy children's clothes are in the wash basket, no favorite meals (most with noodles) await preparation. We succumb to self–pity.

A new stage of parenting awaits. During this stage our children return to ask for advice and share their memories with us. Although our memories differ, they still link the generations together.

These are the rich days of parenting, when we see life fully complemented by the past, the present, and the future.

◊

I will enjoy all the stages of parenting.

_____

_____

_____

_____

_____

January 11

SELF-DOUBT

He (Menachem) was a lovely, healthy baby, and Morris and I were overcome by being parents.

Golda Meier

◊

Overcome. That is how we feel some days. We are overcome by caretaking, responsibilities, and careers. Sometimes we cannot see a flicker of light at the end of the tunnel. Our self–doubt drains us physically and emotionally.

However, it is possible to learn how to turn negative feelings into positive action. We can resolve to take one day at a time. If we still feel overcome, we can take one hour at a time, or one minute. The joys of parenting will come to us.

◊

I will resolve to take one day at a time.

_____

_____

_____

_____

_____

January 12

AMBIVALENCE

We can learn to accept the existence of ambivalent feelings in ourselves and our children.

Dr. Hiam Ginott

◊

The dictionary defines ambivalence as conflicting feelings toward a person or thing. Love and hate are examples of ambivalent feelings. If we are honest with ourselves, we will admit ambivalent feelings make us uneasy.

Having our children disagree with us is painful. We wonder if they ever listened to our kitchen conferences. Our children's ambivalence, however, may be viewed as a marker of success. It tells us our children are thinking, questioning and seeking. Isn't that what we wanted?

◊

I will acknowledge my children's ambivalent feelings.

_____

_____

_____

_____

_____

January 13

PRIDE

Some people make work their personal life, but I choose to have a family. That's my career.

Mia Farrow

◊

Many careers may be open to us, but none seem quite as challenging as parenting. We are surprised to discover that parenting is the toughest career of all. We tire, we question, we falter and these missteps surprise us.

We need to remember we are not alone. There are literally thousands of people with experiences similar to ours. Why don't we talk to each other more? Talking with other parents helps us to anchor our lives. Together, we rejoice in the role life has bestowed upon us. We are parents!

◊

I will take pride in parenting.

_____

_____

_____

_____

_____

January 14

CREATIVITY

There are scarcely two children who express themselves entirely alike.

Viktor Lowenfeld

◊

Fluttering papers, crayon scribbles, water color paintings, wobbly pencil drawings, are stuck to the refrigerator door with magnets. We view them with awe. "Children live here!" the drawings proclaim.

Papers are stuck to refrigerator doors all over town, but none compare with these. These pictures were made by our children. We chuckle at egg-shaped people with stick limbs, purple dogs with long tails, yellow suns with ever–smiling faces.

All of these images are evidence of our children's creativity and make us feel good inside.

◊

I will encourage my children's creativity.

_____

_____

_____

_____

_____

January 15

BIRTHDAYS

Bone of my bones, and flesh of my flesh.
                    Holy Bible, Genesis 2:23

◊

Birthdays flip by like road markers. With each birthday we are more amazed at our children's growth. We have trouble believing our children went off to kindergarten and even more trouble when they enter junior high school. Childhood is passing too quickly.

The excitement of birthdays does not dispel our fear. All of us are "bone of my bones, and flesh of my flesh." A child's birthday also marks our age. We have two choices, to bemoan birthdays or to rejoice them. Let us celebrate the brightly, colored candles. Happy birthday to all!

◊

I will cherish my children's birthdays.

_____

_____

_____

_____

_____

January 16

LOVE

The seed of love must be eternally resown.
                                        Anne Morrow Lindberg
                            ◊

Love is a process of discovery. Our parental love for our children grows so steadily, it surprises us. Just when we thought we could not love our children more, we do. Limitlessly. Forever. Beyond time.

This love blossoms amidst the weeds of illness, conflict, ego, emotion, stress and ignorance. None of these conditions alter the fact that we love our children. The unfailing cycle of family continues, as love for our children intertwines with their love for us.

                            ◊

I will re–plant the seed of love.

_____

_____

_____

_____

_____

January 17

SELF-CARE/ILLNESS

All the children are down and half–down with a virulent cold. Five noses easily seem fifty–five when they are all running at once.

Pearl Buck

◊

If we could, we would gladly suffer a rotten cold, itchy measles, and any other diseases for our children. Our children become ill, anyway. Taking care of sick children can make us feel helpless. It also reminds us of how deeply we love our children.

Worried parents often neglect themselves. In trying to be all things to all people, we deplete our natural reserves. We must take care of ourselves. The kids are going to need us when they bound out of bed!

◊

I will take care of myself.

_____

_____

_____

_____

_____

January 18

EXPRESSIONS

Her face swims before me when she's not there, and I think about her before I go to sleep. I dream about her, and when I wake up I can't wait to see her.

Bette Midler

◊

Our children are such an integral part of us, we cannot stand to be separated from them. Business trips become painful. We want to see, hear, and hug the children we have left behind. "What are they doing now?" we ask.

We may derive comfort from the mental images of our children's faces, eyes crinkled in laughter, lips pursed in disappointment, messy cocoa mouths. There is nothing so changeable—or beautiful—as the face of a child.

◊

I will derive joy from my children's facial expressions and the feelings they convey.

January 19

RESPONSIBILITY

Remember: *With fulfillment comes responsibility.*
                                    Bill Cosby
                          ◊

Unlike the fall television previews, life does not give us parenting previews. Thank goodness. Or else we might conclude we are not up to the task. The ups and downs of parenting bring more responsibilities and we are frightened.

Instead of succumbing to fear, we can take pride in meeting our responsibilities. Keeping the welfare of children paramount, we will do the best we can with each day. That is all anybody can do. We need to take our own advice and not be so hard on ourselves.
                          ◊

I will face the responsibilities of this day.

_____

_____

_____

_____

_____

January 20

LETTING GO

There are only two lasting bequests we can hope to give our children. One of these is roots; the other, wings.

Hodding Carter

◊

When I think about letting go, I always think of Billy, one of my kindergarten students. On the first day of school, Billy's mother put him on the bus, watched the doors close, listened to the engine rev, and started running. The bus driver saw her jouncing form in the rear view mirror.

"She kept up with me pretty well," he said. "When I shifted into second she ran faster. She was still behind me when I shifted into third. I couldn't believe anybody could run that fast."

Clearly, Billy's mother did not want to let go of her son. At the end of the year, however, she wrote me a touching letter, saying Billy had enjoyed kindergarten more than any other child in the class. The successful school year had taught Billy's mother about letting go.

◊

I will work at letting go.

_____

_____

_____

_____

_____

January 21

ADOLESCENCE

As parents, we really need to begin preparing for our children's adolescence when they are in the cradle.

David Elkind

◊

It is hard to believe babies grow up, and surely not taller than their parents. It is also hard to believe our babies will become independent. Our children's quest for independence may lead to adolescent rebellion.

Before adolescence arrives, we can prepare for it. As we watch our children "drive" their tricycles, we will remind ourselves that they will be driving a car soon. We can take the time to learn about adolescence. Slowly, slowly, slowly, we condition ourselves for the years ahead.

Adolescence is difficult for kids and parents.

◊

I will prepare myself for adolescence.

_____

_____

_____

_____

_____

January 22

SELF-LOVE

We must value ourselves as much as we value our children.

Phyllis & David York and Ted Wachtel

◊

Our children are treasures, the most precious ingredient in our lives. But we can get so wrapped up in our children we ignore personal signs of stress. The fun part of parenting fizzles in an instant.

We can recharge our parenting by valuing ourselves. The parents who love themselves tend to raise children who love themselves. So we will think, dream, plan, fantasize, indulge, laugh, explore and challenge. This sounds selfish until we realize our children are doing the same thing.

In order to value ourselves, we must love ourselves.

◊

I will work at self—love.

_____

_____

_____

_____

_____

January 23

COMMUNICATION

If parents would only realize how they bore their children!
George Bernard Shaw

◊

Many of us contract a parenting disease that could be called "repeat–itis." We repeat ourselves constantly, as if sheer repetition could alter our children's behavior. Our children become used to this verbal barrage and tune us out.

It might be better to concede to a difference of opinion at the outset. We can express our opinions to children with measured words. Just like a news bulletin, the brief message is received and remembered.

◊

I will try to express my thoughts concisely.

_____

_____

_____

_____

_____

January 24

ROLE REVERSAL

Like any father, I have moments when I wonder whether I belong to my children or they belong to me.

Bob Hope

◊

What we do for our children is amazing. Right after we explain there is no room for a dog, a yelping puppy is curled up in a cardboard box in the garage. Right after we say we have to do the dishes, we are sitting on the floor playing a game of checkers. Right after we say nobody can spend the night, we are unrolling sleeping bags and making popcorn.

We grumble to our children, but the grumbles are a sham. If we are honest, we will admit that parents, like all people, like to be needed. Reversing roles with our children brings out the adult in them and the child in us. Besides, reversing roles is fun.

◊

I will enjoy reversing roles with my children.

_____

_____

_____

_____

_____

January 25

DEPENDENCE

Only through being first dependent can a child ultimately achieve independence.

Dr. Lee Salk

◊

Babies are dependent beings. Hunger, thirst, cleanliness, warmth, security—every need must be met by parents. At two in the morning we groggily get up for the late—night feeding and diaper change. What a grind.

Another light goes on across the street and we are comforted by its brightness. The neighbors are up with their baby. Lights and babies and parenting link us together in the darkness. We feel a oneness with all parents who are taking care of their children.

◊

I will enjoy my children's dependence while it lasts.

January 26

ACTIONS

Children need to be told constantly—over and over again by their parents—that they are loved.

Princess Grace of Monaco

◊

We tell our children that we love them. Perhaps we have not said the words often enough. Adults need to hear "I love you" repeatedly and children are no different.

Words, alone, cannot express parental love. Love is demonstrated in many ways, holding hands, listening, washing clothes, fixing favorite suppers, riding bikes together. The list is endless. All of these actions remind us of the constancy of love.

◊

I will show love in many ways.

_____

_____

_____

_____

_____

January 27

HELPING/CONTROL

The children always helped their mother to edit my books.
Mark Twain

◊

We get so used to doing things for our children, we forget they can do things for themselves.

Our children can make lunch and fold clothes and run errands and vacuum rugs and rake leaves and feed pets. Perhaps the jobs will not be done the way we would have done them, but they are done.

We need to relinquish some of our control and allow our children to help us. Pulling back helps our children move forward to independence. Isn't independence one of our goals?

◊

I will ask my children for help.

_____

_____

_____

_____

_____

January 28

CARING TIME

I felt about my children as if they were plants.
                                              Jehan Sadat

◊

Working parents find it difficult to give children all the attention they need. Finding time to nurture children in single parent families is even harder. All we can do is try.

We can turn off the television, take the phone off the hook, close the door on outside noise, and focus on our children. Our children are front and center—in the spotlight. Sitting close together, we see each other's facial expressions and feel each other's emotions. Caring flows between us, the parent–child connection that recharges us for the days ahead.

◊

I will set aside time for my children.

_____

_____

_____

_____

_____

January 29

IMMEDIACY/ABILITY

I was devastated by the news (of our daughter's deaf-ness), but determined to help my daughter learn, and grow strong, and lead as normal a life as possible.

Beverly Sills

◊

Having a physically challenged child makes us question the justice of life. We wonder if the disability was our fault and worry how our child will cope in the years ahead. Both questions divert us from the "here" and "now".

Yesterday belongs to the past and cannot be changed. Tomorrow belongs to the future and cannot be foretold. All we have is this day—the immediate. Concentrating on the immediate sets an example for our children. This day was meant to be lived.

◊

I will focus upon the immediate.

_____

_____

_____

_____

_____

January 30

HAPPINESS

It's important to smile.

Robert Conklin

◊

A smile is a powerful thing. The dreary day becomes an exciting challenge, all because of a smile. Children smile easily but sometimes adults have to work at it. There seems to be little to smile about.

Well, we can fake it. Extending facial muscles into a smile makes us feel differently. The smile we bestow upon a stranger creates a ripple of pleasure. Our smiles are returned and we begin to view life optimistically again. Some of us (and we shall be nameless) think our pets smile.

Young children draw smiles on nearly everything. Maybe we should follow their example.

◊

I will find something to smile about today.

_____

_____

_____

_____

_____

January 31

HERITAGE

She is so much like me that she can read my mind at times, which can be most annoying.

Cecil B. DeMille

◊

There are times when our kids annoy us. They whine, argue, postpone, over plan, underachieve and act downright cranky. Worse, there are times when our children seem to read our minds. Do they have x-ray vision?

Because our children's personality traits mirror our own, we quickly recognize them. Seeing the same negative behaviors in our children is worrisome. We must come to terms with the alikeness of our children.

Our children's personality traits are evidence of their heritage. Despite annoying similarities, our children will adapt, change, dream and grow into separate people.

◊

I will accept my children for who they are.

_____

_____

_____

_____

_____

February 1

RULES

Without rules there is no game.

John Dewey

◊

The first time we say "no" to our children is harder on us than it is on them. Seeing our kids pout, cry, scream and throw tantrums makes us cringe.

Setting ground rules for our children is part of parenting. The child who chooses to defy the rules may turn the household into a battleground. No wonder there are days when we think it would be better to forgo rules entirely.

Rules give structure to family life. Children feel safer when they live by the rules and we do, too. Playing by the rules gives our kids a better chance at "winning" the game of life.

◊

I will find the courage to set and enforce rules.

_____

_____

_____

_____

_____

February 2

LONELINESS

My retirement gives me time to spend with our children who, to some extent, are almost friendly strangers to me.
                                        Dr. Charles Mayo

◊

Somehow, when we were not looking, our children grew up and we grew older. "Who are these people?" we ask.

Grown children often have talents and interests different from ours. These differences make us feel lonely.

Parenting adult children forces us to continue adapting to life. Although we nurture from afar, we nurture, nevertheless. This kind of parenting feels strange at first. Then we discover it is another one of life's gifts, filled with surprises and love.

◊

I will take pride in my adult children.

_____

_____

_____

_____

_____

February 3

LEARNING

I once spent the summer thinking of all the things that bothered me—teen pregnancy, drugs, everything—and I realized everything would be better if more people could read and write.

Barbara Bush

◊

We drag ourselves home after a stressful day and what is waiting for us? Homework. Our plans for a quiet evening vanish in an instant.

With a sigh we sit down at the table and try to make sense of the assignment. Our mood changes quickly. It is exciting—and endearing—to watch a young mind struggle to crack the codes of learning.

Books expose our children to the endless world of ideas. Helping our children with their homework is a small price to pay for literacy. Homework goes better if it includes hugs.

◊

I will help my children to learn.

_____

_____

_____

_____

_____

February 4

DEPENDENCE/GRATITUDE

Real maturity calls for an understanding of our need for dependence...

Gloria and Mortimer Feinberg, John J. Tarrant

◊

We tell ourselves—rather smugly—the things we do for our children are legion. This may be true, but parents need to be cautious about over-estimating their importance. In truth, parents and children have a mutually dependent relationship.

So much of our happiness comes from our children. They fill our lives with laughter, impulsiveness, discovery, and wonder. But we are reluctant to thank our children for these gifts. Is it because we feel vulnerable?

Today is the perfect day to thank our children for the happiness they bring to our lives. One sentence is all it takes. Our children will understand the depths of our feelings and fill in the blanks.

◊

I will thank my children today.

_____

_____

_____

_____

_____

February 5

LEAVE–TAKING

The worst part (about campaigning) was saying good-bye to Amy. She was only two, and so dependent on me. I didn't want to miss a single day of her life.

Rosalynn Carter

◊

Sometimes we are forced to choose between our lives and our children's lives. For one reason or another, we have to leave our children. Packing hurriedly, we may not be aware of how painful leave–taking is for our children.

Extra hugs and kisses, a note tucked beneath the pillow, and talking about feelings, all help ease the pain of leave–taking. We can look forward to coming home and our children welcoming us with outstretched arms.

◊

I will ease the pain of leave–taking.

February 6

ROLE MODELS

My general aims for my children were the ones that had been taught to me as a child—high aspirations, honesty, loyalty, and politeness.

Dr. Benjamin Spock

◊

The template for our parenting was drawn by our parents years ago. We need not follow this template, however.

Our willingness to devise new parenting patterns demonstrates a willingness to change. Change is the greatest constant of life. It is possible to change and still adhere to the basic family values which span the generations.

New parenting patterns, like fine spices, add flavor and zest to our lives.

◊

I will craft my own parenting patterns.

_____

_____

_____

_____

_____

February 7

NUTRITION/MEAL–TIME

From my point of view—twenty years after—there are only two kinds of children...picky eaters and...stuffers.

Jean Kerr

◊

Some days we draw a blank on supper. Nothing sounds good. We are tired of fixing meals for picky eaters, stuffers and complainers. If we hear one more complaint about vegetables, we think we'll scream.

Food preparation draws family members together. Tantalizing smells lure our kids into the kitchen. They enjoy baking cookies, tossing salad, stirring pudding, and of course, tasting for flavor.

Come suppertime, the picky eaters, stuffers, and complainers enjoy their food. Our children derive satisfaction from helping us and we derive satisfaction from feeding them properly.

◊

I will prepare balanced meals for my children.

_____

_____

_____

_____

_____

February 8

HAPPINESS/TIME

As parents we have too much to lose by not learning how to enjoy being with our children.

Herbert Kohl

◊

Parenting is time-consuming. Running errands is an ongoing job, as are housework and career. We begin to fantasize about vacations and send for colorful brochures. Vacationing with children takes so much planning and effort, our interest wanes.

Everyone in the family loses if we do not spend time together. We have the option of taking a vacation from life and staying home instead. There are so many things we could do with our children: fly a kite, plant a garden, compile a photo album, plan a game, share our dreams.

Spending time with our children makes them feel cherished.

◊

I will take the time to enjoy my children.

_____

_____

_____

_____

_____

February 9

SELF-AWARENESS/EMPTY–NEST

Learn to get in touch with the silence within yourself and know that everything in this life has a purpose.

Elizabeth Kubler-Ross

◊

The silence of a childless home is deafening. It does not take us long to realize that silence reminds us of loneliness.

Just like the ages and stages of childhood, there are ages and stages of parenting. Having independent children restores freedom to our lives.

Parents need to stay in touch with their feelings if they are to benefit from this freedom. We need to ask ourselves: What do I want to do today? This week? This month? This year?

Instead of postponing our lives, we have the chance to confront each day with the excitement of youth. Life has given us more time to transform dreams into reality.

◊

I will use silence to get in touch with myself.

February 10

RELATIONSHIPS

In trying to keep proving our love for you children, we ran the risk of ceasing to give to each other.

Pearl Bailey

◊

Beneath the hustle and bustle of childcare a trap lies waiting. Taking care of children is so time consuming, there is little time left for us. We may take love for granted and put our personal relationships on hold.

Our days are filled with "if's". If we only had more time. If we only had more money. If we only had fewer responsibilities. If we had chosen a different career. If...

Nobody said we had to ignore our partners in order to be good parents. Children learn about love from us. They need to know that love extends beyond parent-child feelings. Giving to my partner is one of the greatest joys of life.

◊

I will give to my partner today.

_____

_____

_____

_____

_____

February 11

BELIEFS

Yes, children believe plenty of queer things.
                    Oliver Wendell Holmes

◊

On the first day of kindergarten I gathered the class around me for roll–call. When I called Tony's name he burst into tears. "Don't call me that!' he shouted.

As I talked with Tony I realized he did not know his last name. He thought I was criticizing him. I showed Tony the class list, pointing out his first and last names.

"I have two names also," I said. My first name is Harriet and my last name is Hodgson."

Instantly Tony stopped crying. "H–a–r–r–i–e–t?" he asked, stretching out the letters, emphasizing the r's and looking incredulous. Obviously, Tony thought my name was strange.

Tony sat down and smiled. I guess he figured if I could put up with being Harriet, he could put up with being Tony, first name and last.

◊

I will get to know my children's peers.

_____

_____

_____

_____

_____

February 12

ADOLESCENCE

Between the ages of twelve and seventeen a parent can age thirty years.

Sam Levenson

◊

Adolescents should have warning labels on them: This kid may act crazy, disrupt the household, challenge authority and cause severe heartburn in parents.

Just as the other stages of childhood pass, so too, will adolescence. We stand a better chance of surviving adolescence if we arm ourselves with humor. Certainly, a sense of humor can rescue us from a myriad of sticky situations.

Stressful as our children's adolescence may be, we must have some faith in them and concentrate on the big things in life. Like love.

◊

I will love my children during their adolescence.

_____

_____

_____

_____

_____

February 13

WORRY/SPIRITUALITY

. . . even when things are going well, you have to worry that they aren't.

Louise De Grave

◊

Worry begets worry. Those of us who permit our worries to get out of control find our lives are out of control. Is there a solution?

One thing we can do is balance worry with spirituality. In the words of the *Serenity Prayer*, we can work on accepting the things we cannot change, find the courage to change the things that can be changed, and develop the wisdom to know the difference.

Our perception of events affects our happiness. So let us turn our worries over to our Higher Power. A beautiful day awaits us.

◊

I will balance worry with spirituality.

_____

_____

_____

_____

_____

February 14

GIVING

My baby and her best girlfriend gave me valentines as does Bess, and I couldn't get out to buy them one.

Harry Truman

◊

Holidays add to the joy of parenting. We receive valentines cut out with jagged strokes and birthday presents swathed in yards of tape. These loving remembrances bring tears to our eyes.

If we have not had the time to respond in kind, we feel guilty. Guilt drains our energy and can be harmful to us. Nobody can make us feel worse than we do. We must remember the greatest gift we can give our children is love.

◊

I will accept my children's gifts joyfully.

_____

_____

_____

_____

February 15

FIRSTBORN

Perhaps my love for my firstborn was quite ridiculous, perhaps I sounded ridiculous when I wrote about her . . .
                                                                        Fydor Dostoyevsky

◊

At last! Months of waiting culminate in birth and we are awed by this tiny being. The feelings we have for our firstborn are so strong they almost defy description. We babble to complete strangers about the baby's milky burps and wrinkled toes, feeling ridiculous afterwards.

Diaper changes, teething, walking, toilet training and early learning become the lacework of our lives. But familiarity with childcare may dull the miracle of birth. Each child deserves to be treated like the firstborn.

◊

I will treat each of my children like the firstborn.

_____

_____

_____

_____

_____

February 16

SELF-FORGIVENESS

Forgiveness simply means you're ready to let go and move on.

Leonard Felder

◊

It is impossible for the parents of a newborn baby to understand the meaning of the word forgiveness. Experience teaches us that we must forgive our children. However, many of us fail to forgive ourselves.

Memories of our parenting mistakes are stored on mental tape recorders. Replaying the tapes anchors us to the past and mars the present. Parents who have the courage to forgive their children have the courage to forgive themselves.

This day, this moment, let us give ourselves the gift of forgiveness.

◊

I will give myself the gift of forgiveness.

_____

_____

_____

_____

_____

February 17

LETTING GO

...children graduate to the next stage of things... What shall we give them on these occasions? Imagination, a shove out and up, a blessing.

Robert Fulghum

◊

Even confident parents falter when confronted with the first pair of baby shoes, a kindergarten progress report, a string of scout badges, the first date, and kids going off to college. We want to cry but hold our tears inside.

Nature teaches us about letting go. A mother robin, for example, demonstrates flying to her young. If a baby bird refuses to leave the nest, the mother perches on a nearby branch and calls to it. If a baby bird still refuses to leave the nest, the mother gives it a psychological shove by flying away.

Letting go is easier if we give our kids a nudge, a smile and a blessing. Like the mother robin, we have to believe our kids can fly.

◊

I will let go with a nudge, a smile, and a blessing.

_____

_____

_____

_____

_____

February 18

CONNECTIONS

Letting go of our vain expectations as parents . . . we learn to give thanks for even imperfect connections.

Judith Viorst

◊

It comes to us all, a time when children refuse to listen to parental advice. That does not stop us from giving it. We push our vain expectations upon our children. How we persist!

Our alienated children become more alienated, going out as often as possible and responding to questions with grunts. Parent-child connections are shaky and uncomfortable. Although it may not seem like it, this is the perfect time to have faith in our kids. The communication lines are open as long as connections exist.

Love, itself, is an imperfect connection.

◊

I will give thanks for imperfect connections.

_____

_____

_____

_____

_____

February 19

SELF-WORTH

You cannot affirm a child's life if there is no correspond-ing affirmation of your life and needs.

Angela Barron McBride

◊

Some of us are confused. We think we are acting selfishly if we have career ambitions, get absorbed in hobbies, require solitude or want time out from parenting. These are not expressions of selfishness, they are expressions of humanness.

We do not have to explain our needs to our children. Our role models speak for themselves and the message is clear. Parents are people, too, and people have needs. Watching us struggle to meet our needs gives our kids "permission" to meet their needs. Meeting individual needs is an affirmation of life.

◊

I will admit my needs to my children.

_____

_____

_____

_____

_____

February 20

FEELINGS

Children are very sensitive to our inner feelings. They are not easily fooled by words.

Dr. Bruno Bettleheim

◊

Kids are natural detectives. Although we stuff our feelings, or gloss over them, our children know when we are in emotional turmoil. Stuffing our feelings is a disservice to our children, who may feel guilty for their own feelings and try to stuff them.

Honesty is a better policy for children and parents to live by. We can describe feelings to young children in a few words. Even toddlers understand words like tired, rushed, worried and sad. Sharing feelings with our children strengthens the bonds of love.

◊

I will tell my children how I am feeling.

_____

_____

_____

_____

_____

February 21

CONVERSATION

Parents of young children should realize that few people and maybe no one, will find their children as enchanting as they do.

Barbara Walters

◊

Parenting is exciting. But inconsiderate parents feel compelled to talk about their children in endless detail. These parents do not notice the bored facial expressions of their listeners.

We need to think before we speak. Limiting our stories makes the stories we select shine with originality, poignancy and humor. Let us stop yammering about our kids. Listening, observing and meditating are ways of cherishing children, also.

◊

I will limit the stories I tell about my children.

_____

_____

_____

_____

_____

February 22

LISTENING

There isn't a child who hasn't gone out into the brave new world who eventually doesn't return to the old homestead carrying a bundle of dirty clothes.

Art Buchwald

◊

No sooner has our child left for college, when he or she returns with a mountain of laundry. Laundry is not the issue here, life is, and we need to be attuned to this fact.

Many of life's problems are solved while we are doing mundane tasks. Working alongside our children helps us to get in touch with them. A casual aside can tell us more about a child than hours of conversation.

Thank goodness for laundry and all of the other mundane tasks of life. It is listening time again.

◊

I will take the time to listen to my children.

_____

_____

_____

_____

_____

February 23

ACCEPTANCE

How we accept our children has a profound impact on how they accept themselves.

Peggy Finston, M.D.

◊

We want our children to excel—to be shining examples of the kind of "product" we turn out.

My mother was a whiz at math and could not understand my inability. She cut up food for days, toast, coffee cakes, pies, to get me to understand fractions. Part of the problem is that I am not interested in math but prefer artistic projects. I was fortunate to have parents who accepted this.

It is not always easy to accept our children, but it is possible. Acceptance strengthens the love parents and children feel for one another.

◊

I will accept my children's abilities and inabilities.

_____

_____

_____

_____

_____

February 24

SECURITY

The child who experiences comfortable love and security in his crucial relationships during his growing years will tend to look forward to later relationships with other people . . .
                                        Dr. A. H. Chapman

◊

How can we build secure lives for children in an insecure world? Change is the very fabric of our lives, woven into our days, seasons and years.

Our children's feelings of security are determined, in great part, by our attitudes about change. If we accept change as normal, our children will do the same. If we view change as an opportunity for growth, our children will do the same. If we celebrate the changes of life, our children will do the same.

When we accept change, we feel more secure about life. And parenting.

◊

I will help my child to accept change.

_____

_____

_____

_____

_____

February 25

PEACEFULNESS

Sleep my child and peace attend thee, all through the night.

Sir Harold Boulton

◊

Putting children to bed is a poignant experience. Exhausted as we are, we are energized by the love we have for our children.

The once tumultuous house is quiet. Now we have time for ourselves. How easy it is to dwell upon the negatives of the day, rather than the positives. Images and questions and conflicts invade our thoughts.

Stop doing this, we tell ourselves, but how? We can set aside some quiet time, pick a single thought, and focus upon it. Serenity may be found in the peaceful moments of life.

◊

I will savor the peaceful moments of life.

_____

_____

_____

_____

_____

February 26

PAIN

I'll remember to respect her pain by not trying to cure it.
Ellen Walker

◊

We want the best for our children. Imbued with the desire to give our children perfect lives, we become overprotective and shield them from pain.

This is unfair to all family members. Children learn to deal with pain by experiencing it. They must learn to make their own decisions, live with these decisions, and modify their behavior.

To live is to feel pain. As difficult as it is, we can show respect for our children by letting them feel—and deal with—their pain.

◊

I will let my children learn from pain.

_____

_____

_____

_____

_____

February 27

SERENITY

We may take something like a star, to stay our minds on and be staid.

Robert Frost

◊

As youngsters, many of us made wishes when we looked at the stars. This child-like impulse can comfort us today.

Away from the glare of city lights, we are able to gaze at the heavens and see billions of twinkling stars. If we are lucky, we might see a shooting star. We are awed by thoughts of other galaxies, endless space, advanced technology, time travel and alternate forms of life.

Compared to the stars, we are insignificant. However, we can find a measure of serenity in looking at the heavens and wishing on the first star of the evening.

◊

I will turn to nature for serenity.

_____

_____

_____

_____

_____

February 28

CHILDHOOD

When I stop writing about children, I still insist on writing about people who were children once.

A. A. Milne

◊

Sometimes we forget we were ever children. According to respected psychologists, the adults who retain some child-like qualities enjoy life more.

Sharing memories with children helps them to see the child which resides within us. We smile at the similarities in our lives, the joy of singing, munching warm cookies, snuggling beneath clean sheets.

Today is an ideal day to give in to our impulses and reveal the child that lives inside us. Our kids are in for a surprise!

◊

I will share my childhood memories with my children.

_____

_____

_____

_____

_____

February 29

COMPULSION

Having ceased being such a compulsive instructor, I find there is more room in my life for other kinds of parenthood.
                                        Phyllis Theroux

◊

There is no rule that says parents have to be instructors. True, some parents make good instructors, but the role was not assigned to us.

Rather than instructing, we can parent by example, play, role reversal, time out, whatever comes to mind. Our children see we are adaptive people, eager to do our best.

We have left compulsive instruction behind and entered the age of creative parenting.

◊

I will guard against compulsive parenting.

_____

_____

_____

_____

_____

March 1

MATURITY

Maturity: among other things, the unclouded happiness of a child at play, who takes it for granted that he is at one with his playmates.

Dag Hammarskjold

◊

A child is completely happy sitting in a pile of sand with nothing but a cup and spoon.

Unlike our children, many of us neglect the play aspect of our lives. We are convinced there is no time for play. If we are to be good providers for our children, we must keep working, working, working.

Mature adults, however, recognize the need for time out. Playing with our children connects us with them as nothing else can. Play tells our children that we trust life.

◊

I will take time out for play.

_____

_____

_____

_____

_____

March 2

FEELINGS

> Children and adults are best able to choose constructive
> actions when they can label their feelings accurately...
>
> Michael Schulman and Eva Mekler

◊

Sometimes labels help. Labeling our feelings helps our children to understand us. A straightforward, "I'm feeling grouchy," begins the process.

Once we label our feelings, we need to take the time to explain the reasons for these feelings. Not only does this mental exercise help our children, it helps us. Everyone in the family feels better when feelings are out in the open.

Of course we need to be prudent about labeling, but sometimes labels are just what families need.

◊

I will label my feelings for my children.

_____

_____

_____

_____

_____

March 3

LEARNING

Guiding without pulling makes the process of learning gentle.

Confucious

◊

Centuries ago, Confucious discovered that gentle learning was more successful than pressured learning.

Think back to your childhood. Are there special times of learning that stand out in your memory? What made them special for you? Can these times be replicated with your children?

We want our children to learn. Zealousness, however, sometimes causes us to push our children. Forget pushing. Try gentle guidance and hugs, a la Confucious.

◊

I will gently guide my children's learning.

_____

_____

_____

_____

_____

March 4

ATTITUDE

Henceforth I ask not good—fortune, I myself am good-fortune.

Walt Whitman

◊

Alcohol, drugs, sex, pregnancy, AIDS, we have plenty to worry about. Conversations with other parents contain such phrases as "squeaking by," "avoiding trouble" and "being lucky." It sounds as if we are expecting problems.

Researchers have discovered negative talk can lead to negative thinking, especially if the talk is repeated. In *Song of the Open Road*, Walt Whitman wrote about a *"positive attitude"*—a feeling of self that led to good fortune.

We have had the good fortune to become parents. Instead of living in fear, let us live in hope.

◊

I will focus on the positives of parenting.

_____

_____

_____

_____

_____

March 5

HAPPINESS

Now, it is my time to be happy. Won't you celebrate with me?

Roseanne Barr

◊

Parents want to be happy. It turns out happiness is an elusive emotion. What is happiness, anyway?

The smallest things in life make us happy. We feel happy when a baby coos at us. We feel happy when a child draws a picture for us. We feel happy when a child gives us a sticky kiss.

Happiness is not so much a right as it is an attitude. We are in charge of our own happiness. During sad times, we may find comfort in happy memories. Happy memories, in turn, can be a springboard to happy thoughts.

◊

I will think about happy things today.

_____

_____

_____

_____

_____

March 6

DISCIPLINE

Discipline itself must be disciplined.

M. Scott Peck, M.D

◊.

Sooner or later every child must be disciplined. A toddler who runs in front of a car, for example, needs to be disciplined immediately and firmly.

Discipline can be frightening. Parents feel as if they are squeezed in a vice between responsibility and children's freedom. Much as we helped our children learn to walk, we help them to learn self-control.

Our parenting is easier if we think of discipline as a positive influence in our children's lives. Discipline includes trust, negotiation, parent-child contracts and applied humor. In short, we love our kids enough to discipline them.

◊

I will consider the positive aspects of discipline.

_____

_____

_____

_____

_____

March 7

QUIET TIME

I am certain that any child who does not take tap dancing and tennis lessons will end up in analysis.
                    Caryl Rivers and Alan Lupe
◊

Somehow we develop the notion that a child who takes lessons will succeed in life. Now there's a definite maybe!

While lessons help our children develop their innate talents, the lessons should not be more important than the kids who take them. We do not need to plan every minute of a child's day. One of the most thoughtful things we can do for our children is to give them quiet time.

Our children need time to think, time to let their imaginations run riot, and time to listen to their dreams. Learning how to handle quiet time is a lesson in life.
◊

I will make sure my children have quiet times.

_____

_____

_____

_____

_____

March 8

IMMEDIACY

I cherish the days as they roll by . . .

                                        Tom Bodett

◊

Do you live life like a freeway driver speeding past everything you encounter?

Some of us welcome the blur. To avoid the pain of life, we keep our schedules full and our pace full-out. We are determined to be busy people. However, the strongest will cannot alter the course of events.

We need to accept the unhappy, painful events of life and move on. Beautiful days await us.

◊

I will cherish this day, no matter what it brings.

_____

_____

_____

_____

_____

March 9

HAPPINESS

Look to this day! For it is life.
                          Ancient Sanskrit poem
                    ◊

It takes courage to enjoy life, not the courage of battle, but the courage of acceptance. We need to accept life for what it is and what it is not. Some days we feel euphoric. Other days we feel despair. We must not allow despair to rule our lives.

There are many things to be happy about, if we examine our lives closely. Nothing that happens, including the death of family members, can erase the love we feel for our children. Let us anticipate this day that is so filled with life.

                    ◊

I will anticipate this day of parenting.

_____

_____

_____

_____

_____

March 10

TRADITION

We create our own traditions for the same reason we create our own families. To know where we belong.

Ellen Goodman

◊

Family traditions are fun. The traditions we have do not have to be serious ones, but can be downright silly.

My father–in–law started a hilarious tradition. He always wore a battered derby hat while he recycled the water softener. The hat was supposed to remind Dad to turn off the machine. Long after the softener had shut off, Dad was often still wearing the hat. Dad's family tradition evokes smiles to this day.

New traditions make us feel closer to our children.

◊

I will start new traditions with my children.

_____

_____

_____

_____

_____

March 11

EQUALITY

A parent should never make distinctions between his children.

The Talmud

◊

Our children have varying abilities. One child may be a natural athlete, whereas another child may be a natural artist. These disparate talents can lead to jealousy, anger, and family distinctions.

Although our children do not possess equal talents, they deserve equal opportunities. If the artist wants to go out for sports, so be it. This trial and answer process helps a child to come to terms with the age-old question, "Who am I?"

◊

I will treat my children equally.

_____

_____

_____

_____

_____

March 12

VALUES

It is only with the heart that one can see rightly...
                                    Antoine De Saint-Exupery
◊

Clear as they are to us, parental values can be invisible to children. That is why we need to make our values clear.

Children will think our values are more credible if we support them with facts. The parent who asks a child to stop smoking, for example, needs to explain how smoking affects health, fertility, the unborn and non–smokers. But facts alone will not sway a child.

Our values are based on feelings, too. Let us say the words we are thinking. Feeling words are powerful words, just the ones to communicate our values.
◊

I will discuss values with my children.

_____

_____

_____

_____

_____

March 13

SELF-DISCOVERY

The main task of parenthood is to be oneself, to work at self-discovery.

Eda L. Le Shan

◊

Parenthood does not mean the end of personhood. In fact, it is just the opposite. As our children discover themselves, we also discover ourselves. Every age and stage of parenting contains exciting discoveries.

It turns out that self-discovery and life-discovery are parallel processes. Our children will continue to make discoveries, just as we have. We are never too old to surprise ourselves. How can you surprise yourself today?

◊

I will continue to learn about myself.

_____

_____

_____

_____

_____

March 14

PERCEPTION

Parenthood is an unmatched opportunity for growing in beauty and creativity.

Polly Berrien Berends

◊

Countless artists have tried to draw like children. Few have succeeded. Because children have no preconceived ideas about size, color and form, their drawings explode with originality.

Our children can find beauty amidst the most bleak surroundings. Parenting gives us another chance to experience childhood, to see life through the eyes of a child. Along with our children, we have unlimited opportunities to grow in beauty and creativeness.

What a blessing!

◊

I will view life through the eyes of a child.

_____

_____

_____

_____

_____

March 15

CONNECTEDNESS

I seem to enjoy a warm glow at the idea of helping to people the earth.

E. B. White

◊

When we became parents, we joined an international network of mothers and fathers. The warm glow of parenting unites us and the specter of war haunts us.

Perhaps the greatest chance for lasting peace lies with parents. No matter what nationality we are, we want better lives for our children. We are the voices of peace. Working together, we have the power to change policies and topple governments.

Mother-to-mother, father-to-father, we work for peace in diverse ways. Exposing our children to other cultures keeps the flame of peace alight.

◊

I will expose my children to other cultures.

_____

_____

_____

_____

_____

March 16

AGING

What an advantage we have over our children! While they, to their embarrassment, grow up—voices changing, legs and arms becoming too obvious...we gracefully, comfortably, grow down.

Joyce Kilmer

◊

Elderly people are revered in the Chinese culture. According to the Chinese, the elderly are not old people, they are gold people, rich in experience and wisdom.

There are many positive aspects to aging. Awareness of aging makes us appreciate the moment. No surprise, then, that somebody started the trend of putting nursery schools in nursing homes.

Gracefully the aging grow down and impulsively the children grow up. The two age groups share a wonder of life. Like spring buds, every day is bursting with possibilities.

◊

I will grow older with dignity.

_____

_____

_____

_____

_____

March 17

CHANGE

*I wonder if I've been changed in the night? I almost think
I can remember feeling a little different.*

Lewis Caroll

◊

Children change quickly. We change quickly, too,
although we may not notice it. In the morning, we wake up
feeling different. Our minds were working overtime in
the night.

Ready or not, change came to us. We can track the
evolution of change by retracing our steps. The Serenity
Prayer asks for acceptance of the things we cannot change.
Fighting change is a waste of effort. We may as well
embrace change, deal with it and move on.

If nothing else, change keeps life from becoming
boring.

◊

I will embrace the changes of life.

March 18

PRIORITIES

May you live in interesting times.

Ancient Chinese Curse

◊

All of us have times when too much is happening. Our lives shake like an airplane buffeted by wind gusts. How can we level off?

We can take two simple steps. First, we get in touch with ourselves. Second, we get in touch with our lives. Daily meditation helps us to feel calm again, better equipped to face the future. The quietness of meditation has positive affects on our health.

"First things first" is an Al-Anon slogan. Before we plan anything, we need to figure out our priorities. Setting priorities helps us to handle our every day lives. Serenity comes to those who seek it.

◊

I will set some priorities.

_____

_____

_____

_____

_____

March 19

CHOICES

It is while youth is making its choice that it is at its most fascinating and rewarding, even if parents tend to sigh with relief when that choice is made.

Peter Ustinov

◊

The choices our kids make can make us wince. However, our children will not learn how to make choices if we make their choices for them.

Painful as it is, we need to let our children make their own decisions. Let them buy dumb stuff, plan too much, and form damaging relationships. In time, our children should learn how to take responsibility for their choices.

Inwardly we sigh with relief after some choices have been made, but it might be better to forgo any displays of relief. Our children will make choices more easily if we show confidence in them.

◊

I will encourage my children to make their own choices.

_____

_____

_____

_____

_____

March 20

SELF-RELIANCE

*What you try to do when you raise kids is surround them
with the right kind of thinking so they can function in the world.*
Jim Henson

◊

Self-reliance is an earned quality, developed and
honed by life experience. We cannot learn self-reliance for
our children, but we can foster its development.

Chances are good, if our children are surrounded
by kindness, fairness, tolerance, and morality, they will
apply this thinking to life. These values gird self-reliance
throughout our children's adulthood.

Fostering self-reliance in our children has its
price—namely letting go. That sounds like a fair trade-off.

◊

I will foster my children's self-reliance by letting go.

March 21

TIME

. . . meanings of time we learn only from children.
                                              Harold Witt

◊

Children have their own time systems. A two-year-old will spend an hour looking at a worm. Everything about the worm, from its straight shape to the way it wiggles, is exciting.

We learn the true meaning of time from children. They focus their attention on the wonder of the moment. Most parents do not have the luxury of ignoring time, but we can become more aware of kids' time.

There are many marvelous things to see and do. We simply need to make time for them. If not now, when?

◊

I will meld my meaning of time with my children's.

_____

_____

_____

_____

_____

March 22

PERSONALITY

Children are different—mentally, physically, spiritually, quantitatively and furthermore, they're a little bit nuts.

Jean Kerr

◊

From a purely adult perspective, kids seem to be a little bit nuts. At least some parents think so.

Our children will pay a game for hours and declare everyone the winner. Their drawings defy all the rules of gravity and color, and they invent ridiculous words to meet their conversational needs.

Children's nuttiness is actually naturalness, the uncensored expression of thoughts and deeds. Living with our children's natural personalities makes life an adventure.

◊

I will delight in my children's nuttiness.

_____

_____

_____

_____

_____

March 23

CALMNESS

We have to cut down our activity to the point where we think calmly and reasonably about our actions.

Thomas Merton

◊

Are you a martyr? Some of us get so involved in our children's activities, we have no time for our own activities. Meals are eaten on the run, household maintenance is slap-dash, and we never seem to catch up. Constant running makes us feel run down.

This kind of manic behavior can impede rational thought. Several years ago a popular song advised listeners to "stop and smell the roses." If you are a candidate for martyrdom, you need to stop and consider your actions. Less can be more, especially when it comes to parenting.

◊

I will think about my actions calmly and honestly.

_____

_____

_____

_____

_____

March 24

STRESS

It takes strength to handle the painful tensions of unanswered questions, especially if you have a family.

Charles R. Swindoll

◊

Life is a series of questions.

Parents have questions for their children and children have questions for their parents. Not knowing the answers to questions can make us feel stressed.

We need not be ashamed of the answer, "I don't know." Instead of answering, we can give our children leads to follow. Our children learn that finding the answers to questions is an exciting game. The longer we live, the more questions we ask.

◊

I will have the courage to say, "I don't know."

_____

_____

_____

_____

March 25

ANGER

Anger is neither legitimate nor illegitimate, meaningful nor pointless. Anger simply is.

Harrier Goldhor Lerner, Ph.D.

◊

Kids get angry, but parents? Many of us think we are not supposed to get angry, that we have to be in control at all times. This theory ignores the facts.

All human beings feel anger. Physicians know it is unhealthy to ignore angry feelings. Anger that has no-where to go, that is buried deep within us, can quickly turn into depression. Handling depression can be worse than handling anger.

So let it out. Describe your anger with words and work it off with exercise. We can accept and re—channel the anger within us.

◊

I will acknowledge the anger within me.

_____

_____

_____

_____

_____

March 26

CHILDCARE

Parents are people who bear children, bore teenagers, and board newlyweds.

Anonymous

◊

Parenting is a lifetime commitment. Long before we became parents, we knew this, but we did not live it. Other parents can give us their advice for surviving the so-called terrible twos, nerve wracking piano scales, adolescent rebellion, lonely college years and children's marriages. All we need to do is ask.

Sharing stories about childcare bonds us with other parents. We are not alone.

◊

I will ask other parents about childcare.

_____

_____

_____

_____

_____

March 27

FAMILY

I like pondering the great chain of loving that has gone on and will continue to go on between parents and their children.

Elizabeth Berg

◊

Love links families together; it is a continuous chain. The family talents, concerns, values and traditions are passed on from parent to child.

Families are ongoing by nature and the thought is comforting. Nothing else matters—wealth, accolades, fame—as much as family.

Today's families are spread far and wide. Thousands of miles separate the family members. We can connect with our loved ones by telephone, mail, computer, and old-fashioned story telling. Telling stories about our family is a way of preserving history.

◊

I will tell family stories to my children.

_____

_____

_____

_____

_____

March 28

WORK

I am so happy that my daughter is able to see my hospital. She is delighted with the six chimpanzees and the five young antelopes that play around the yard.

Albert Schweitzer

◊

Children can be bewildered by our work.

To help them understand our work, we can share it with them. We must do this carefully, however, sharing just enough and not too much. Our kids do not need to be burdened by work-related problems. After all, this is our work, not theirs.

Our children will be happier, knowing where we are and what we are doing. Work is a vital part of our lives. We are better parents because of our work. We are better workers because we are parents.

◊

I will share things about my work with my children.

_____

_____

_____

_____

_____

March 29

FAILURE

It is important to fail and important to give our children permission to fail.

Carole Hyatt and Linda Gottleib

◊

As hard as it is to believe, there are good failures. A failure is good if we have learned something from it and grown spiritually. But the goodness of failure is not always apparent. We may have to look hard to find it.

Our children benefit from watching failure in progress. The way they handle failure is based upon the way we handle it. Handling failure openly gives our children permission to fail, also.

According to computer experts, we learn more from negative feedback than we do from positive feedback. Negative feedback forces us to change our tactics. That is why we need to share our failures with children and give them permission to blow it.

◊

I will let my children see me fail.

_____

_____

_____

_____

_____

March 30

CONSTANCY

Constancy is also the reconciliation of our everlasting longing for perfection and our down-to-earth daily existence.

Louise J. Kaplan, Ph.D.

◊

Child experts may disagree on the definition of constancy, but they would probably agree that constancy gives children psychological support.

Constancy is like home plate in a baseball game. When our children are home, supported by our constancy, they feel safe. Running the bases of life is easier for children if they have the secure feelings that come with constancy.

Providing constancy for our children requires hard work and persistence. In short, we need to be constant about constancy.

◊

I will give my children the psychological support of constancy.

_____

_____

_____

_____

_____

March 31

PLAY

We can, as parents . . . restore to the young children now growing up their right and their ability to play for their lives.

Maria W. Piers and Genieve Millet

◊

We live in a whiz-bang world where children are used to boom boxes and computers.

Technical advances are infringing upon our children's rights, specifically the right to play. This right is rapidly disappearing as we buy more high-tech items for our children. Any time our children spend in creative play is time well spent. Play teaches our children about fairness, sharing, problem-solving, planning and more.

Won't you ensure the right of play to your children?

◊

I will ensure the right of play to my children.

_____

_____

_____

_____

_____

April 1

ACCEPTANCE

Accept the fact that there will be moments when your children hate you.

Ann Landers

◊

Being the target of our children's rage comes as a shock to parents, an April Fool's joke gone awry. We cannot understand how our sweet children turned nasty. Where did we go wrong?

We didn't.

Children try out emotions as they grow and hate is one of them. We test our emotions also. If the truth were known, sometimes we have been so angry at our kids we came close to hating them back.

Parents need to take children's emotions in stride and accept them for what they are—part of growing up.

◊

I will consider my children's hateful moments as a part of growing up.

_____

_____

_____

_____

_____

April 2

VALUES

It's how you live your life that counts.

Ryan White

◊

Life does not run on the ration system. After a ration of sadness, we are not assured a ration of happiness. Experiences come to us with the capriciousness of the wind, changing direction and force.

Predicting life experiences is impossible. So how we live our lives is what really counts. We can help our children build the kinds of values which will sustain them in hard times: love, kindness, caring, giving, work, faith.

We can also celebrate life by living it to the fullest.

◊

I will live each day to the fullest.

_____

_____

_____

_____

_____

April 3

BEHAVIOR

Children and princes will quarrel for trifles.
                                        Benjamin Franklin

◊

Our children quarrel over trifles and suck us into their silly arguments. This is a futile experience if there ever was one.

We would do better to save our adrenaline for real crises, and let our children face the consequences of their behavior. Instead of using us as referees, our children will be forced to resolve their own differences. The children who learn to negotiate while they are young will be inclined to practice it when they are grown.

Let us close our eyes and ears to stupid quarrels.

◊

I will ignore stupid quarrels.

_____

_____

_____

_____

_____

April 4

COPING

I could cope with my family very well if only I could take them by appointment.

Phyllis Naylor

◊

Tired or not, busy or not, worried or not, every day we respond to our children's needs. Some days we feel stretched to the limit, ready to snap like an old rubber band.

Coping with children is easier if we meet with them individually. The Al–Anon slogan "One Day At A Time" can be adapted to "One Child At A Time." We might have to make appointments with busy high–schoolers, but it is worth the effort.

Spending one–to–one time with children draws us closer together. Problems shrink. Laughter heals. Dreams emerge. Together, we are coping.

◊

I will cope with my children individually.

_____

_____

_____

_____

_____

April 5

JOY

When everything is over for me and I am an old lady, let me watch kids rehearse in a darkened room.

Joan Rivers

◊

Have you ever watched kids rehearse? They run through scene after scene with boundless energy, confident of success.

This energy stems from a joy of life. From plays to pizza, our children find everything exciting and can hardly wait for the next experience. While our children's joy is amazing, their willingness to share this joy is even more amazing.

Our children share joy freely. It floats into the air with the purity of a robin's song.

◊

I will absorb my children's joy of life.

_____

_____

_____

_____

_____

April 6

BEAUTY

The father in the architect took the children's future to heart in that I wanted them to grow up in beautiful surroundings. I intended them to be infected by a love for the beautiful.

Frank Lloyd Wright

◊

Decorating a child's room can be costly and tiring. Our efforts are more than parental love, but demonstrate artistic appreciation.

Young children are keenly aware of beauty. If you ask preschoolers to sort pictures of beautiful things from pictures of ugly things, they do it in an instant, without any hesitation. And the kids will give you good reasons for their choices.

There is enough ugliness in the world. It is never too early to expose our children to beauty. Hopefully, they will create beautiful spaces for their children.

◊

I will infect my child with a love of beauty.

_____

_____

_____

_____

_____

April 7

PERSONHOOD

Being a mother is what I think has made me the person I am.

Jacqueline Kennedy Onassis

◊

It is difficult to define personality and even more difficult when you factor in parenting.

Most of us are honest enough to admit parenting has changed us. Our children lead us in new directions and sometimes on a merry chase. Being a parent has brought us laughter, happiness, new interests, challenges and goals. Parenting not only enriches our lives, it defines who we are and who we will become.

The impossible becomes possible. We grow in ways we never dreamed.

◊

I will let parenting enrich my personality.

_____

_____

_____

_____

_____

April 8

INVOLVEMENT

It's no secret kids like to pretend they're grown up.
                    Linda Albert and Michael Popkin
◊

Take time to remember.

Do you remember when your child took his first steps? Do you remember when your child dressed up in your clothes? Do you remember when your child talked just like you? Do you remember when your child pretended to have your job?

Kids love pretending they are grown up. Role playing is important to personality development. Although we know this, we are reluctant to include our children in adult activities. We worry about having demanding and over-tired children. Maybe we are over-tired ourselves.

Including our children in adult activities is worth the effort. The day could turn into pure serendipity.
◊

I will include my children in adult activities.

_____

_____

_____

_____

_____

April 9

VISUALIZATION

Try to see your children as whole and complete . . . as though they are already what they can become.

Dr. Wayne Dyer

◊

Teachers try to visualize children as adults. We have difficulty with this visualization because we are too close to our children. This need not stop us from considering their futures, however.

The community people who interact with our children, religious educators, scout leaders, music teachers and coaches, often see them differently. Their insights can affect the way we parent our children.

We can consider these insights and still have dreams for our children. Sometimes dreams come true.

◊

I will let dreams for my children influence my parenting.

_____

_____

_____

_____

_____

April 10

PERSONALITY

There is often an irritability in me which . . . makes me say cross and odious things I don't myself believe.

Queen Victoria

◊

Who likes feeling irritable? Nobody, not even Queen Victoria, who described her grouchiness in the letters she wrote to family members. All of us have times when we blurt out things we do not mean and feel foolish afterwards. We can act more like children than our children.

Parents are not answering machines. We do not have to jump into every conversation or answer every question that is asked. "I need some time to think about that," is an honest and effective reply. And we can take our own advice.

We tell our children to think before they speak. Can we do any less?

◊

I will think before I speak.

_____

_____

_____

_____

_____

April 11

ASSESSMENT

There are times to take inventory.

Jim Klobuchar

◊

Chasing wisdom is like chasing a fast, elusive, zigzagging jackrabbit. Wisdom is always over the next horizon.

Nevertheless we seek wisdom. There are times to be honest with ourselves and take a parenting inventory. Where did we succeed? Where did we fall short? Where could we improve? Children can help us with our parenting assessments but we need to factor age into their responses.

An angry teenager may view our personal assessments as a chance to retaliate. On the other hand, very young children often possess the wisdom of Solomon. They know what counts and can describe it to us in 10 words or less.

◊

I will take honest parenting inventories.

_____

_____

_____

_____

_____

April 12

COMMUNICATION

Practicing the art of silence is one of the most difficult disciplines in the world.

Pat Holt and Dr. Grace Ketterman

◊

Silence is rare in this loud, amplified world. Some of us are unnerved by silence. We think of it as a void that must be filled.

Speech teachers consider silence, the effective pause and use of gestures, as part of communication. Being silent takes guts, especially when our children are opposing us. When we are silent, our children have the chance to hear their own thoughts.

Our silence shows we have faith in our children.

◊

I will communicate with my children using silence.

_____

_____

_____

_____

_____

April 13

LEARNING

Anything which parents have not learned from experiences they can now learn from their children.

Anonymous

◊

Children are natural teachers. They do not waste words or actions, but get right to the heart of the matter. Take a moment to think about the things you have learned from your children.

Because our children differ, the lessons we have learned differ. Learning from our children is exhilarating, as exciting as a roller coaster ride. Our children's experiences meld with our experiences.

If we are to learn from our children, we must hold fast to the child within us and never let go.

◊

I will learn from my children.

_____

_____

_____

_____

_____

April 14

COURAGE

We not only want to help pave the way for our children to come back to us, but we want to have the courage and flexibility to go to our children.

Sharon Strassfeld and Kathy Green

◊

There are days when nothing seems to go right, especially parent-child connections, and arguments abound.

Our children are convinced they are right. We are convinced they are wrong. It looks as if the twain shall never meet. But parents and kids may disagree and still maintain their dignity. We do it by keeping our voices low, agreeing that we disagree, and giving our opponent a way out.

Tomorrow things may be quite different. Can we find the courage to apologize to our children? Can we find the courage to respect their differences of opinion? Can we find the courage to love children who refuse to learn from our experience?

◊

I will swallow pride and return to my children.

_____

_____

_____

_____

_____

April 15

PAIN

When we cling to pain we end up punishing ourselves.
Leo F. Buscaglia, Ph.D.

◊

The human mind stores countless facts every day. These memory chunks are cued up at the darnedest times. Smelling pizza may remind us of painful arguments we have had with our children.

Memories can haunt us. We punish ourselves over and over again. Remembered pain equals the pain of the original experience. However, our memory-pain cycles can have positive results. We can come to terms with our memories, learn from them and set new goals in life.

Clinging to pain is a waste of effort. We have better things to do with our time—and our lives.

◊

I will take conscious steps to recover from pain.

_____

_____

_____

_____

_____

April 16

PERSPECTIVE

Try to keep your perspective...not for a term or for a year but for a lifetime.

Mary Susan Miller

◊

Being too close to a problem can make our vision blurry. Only part of the problem is visible and we cannot see that very well. We do not see how the problem affects family dynamics.

When problems seem insurmountable, we need to step back and view them from a different perspective. Time has a way of healing problems, or at least, minimizing them. It has taken time for the problems to develop and it will take time to solve them.

Parenting is a lifetime commitment. The problems we have with our children will be solved during successful school terms, the cycle of seasons, the maturation of children, the tempering of experience.

◊

I will try to keep my perspective when things get crazy.

_____

_____

_____

_____

_____

April 17

SELF-CARE

We must simply decide that there will be time, regular, consistent and guaranteed, not only for our children but for ourselves.

Phyllis Theroux

◊

Some of us consider parenting an all-or-nothing experience. The members of the "all group" believe they have to spend every minute of the day with their kids. Their compulsive behavior borders on addiction.

How can we take care of children if we cannot take care of ourselves?

Those of us who take care of ourselves feel better mentally and physically. Our kids are happier, too, because we have shown some common sense. When you think about it, self-care is not a selfish act, it is a gift to all family members.

◊

I will take care of myself on a regular basis.

_____

_____

_____

_____

_____

April 18

CHILDCARE

For a while I was convinced that parenthood equalled socks.

Phil Donahue

◊

At the end of the day, we look with satisfaction at a clean house, folded laundry and supper simmering on the stove. We feel good about these accomplishments. However, we need to separate the mechanics of childcare from parental love.

More than paired socks, parenting includes hugs, listening, laughter and praise. We must give our children real praise, and lots of it. A short comment, spoken from the heart, can last a child a lifetime.

◊

I will separate childcare tasks from parental love.

_____

_____

_____

_____

_____

April 19

PATIENCE

Life is filled with the lessons of waiting but the hardest may be when we have to wait for ourselves.

Eugene Kennedy

◊

Teaching a child how to tie his or her shoes takes patience and we are patient. "Just keep practicing," we say, tying the bow loops repeatedly.

Learning how to parent takes patience and we are impatient. We set unrealistic goals and expect instant results. Life may be filled with lessons about waiting, but we do not apply these lessons to ourselves.

Not all parents learn patience. Spring is the time of growth and hope, a good time to practice our patience. We need to be as patient with ourselves as we are with our children, lest we stumble over our untied shoes.

◊

I will strive to be patient with myself.

_____

_____

_____

_____

_____

April 20

ROLES

Parents sometimes end up playing parent with their children rather than being real people with them.

Donald Medeiros, Barbara Porter, I. David Welch

◊

Are you understudying for the role of *parent*? Some of us act that way. We say parent-like things, measuring words and holding back on emotions until opening night. Today is opening night!

The parent–child drama plays every day. Children expect nothing less than reality from us—real emotions from real people. Sometimes our children want us to act like rollicking, spontaneous playmates.

Give in to your childish impulses and verbalize those sappy jokes. The kids will love you for it.

◊

I will act like a real person.

_____

_____

_____

_____

_____

April 21

FAMILY

We rapidly found out that two kids are ten times more trouble than one.

Willie Nelson

◊

Numbers do make a difference. Parenting a large family requires the skill of an international diplomat.

We need to be good time managers, attuned to group dynamics, foster personal growth and nurture talents. These tasks are in addition to feeding, clothing and sheltering our children. How can we do it?

Children can learn to help themselves and each other. Some parents depend upon the buddy system, making an older sibling responsible for a younger one. This kind of partnership between parents and children unites the family.

Our children discover they are not helpless, but helpful in many practical ways.

◊

I will give my children the satisfaction of helping.

_____

_____

_____

_____

_____

April 22

MEMORIES

Then as we struggle on, the thoughts of that peaceful past time of childhood comes to us like soft music and a blissful vision through the snow.

◊

Childhood memories affect our parenting. These memories, which often get rosier with age, can make us try too hard with our children. We wind up spoiling them.

Giving presents to our children is one way of expressing love. There are other expressions of love, such as planning a special trip or experience, a blissful vision our children will remember when they are grown.

Planning special times for our children adds to the beauty of life. We are creating the stuff of memories.

◊

I will plan some blissful times for my children.

_____

_____

_____

_____

_____

April 23

TALENT

Children need to see things done well.

                                        John Holt

◊

Ridiculous as it sounds, there are parents who hide personal talents from their children. They deny their talents because they do not want their children to feel intimidated.

These parents tend to praise their children falsely. Excessive praise undermines our children's self-confidence. Our children need to see things done well if they are going to learn how to judge good work from poor, real talent from dabbling.

Using our talents is not vanity, it is thankfulness for what we have been given. Sharing these talents with our children can help them appreciate their own talents and gives them career leads for the future.

◊

I will admit my talents and share them with my children.

_____

_____

_____

_____

_____

April 24

FRIENDSHIP

Each friendship has its own special quality.
               Christine Leefeldt and Ernest Callenback
                              ◊

A friend can change the day.

     Having a friend to share our experiences with can be the difference between enduring a day and embracing a day. However, we can get so involved in our children's friendships that we neglect our own.

     It takes time to maintain friendships and time is something we are always short of. Our children will mature and leave us, whereas our friends will probably remain. Put the care and feeding of friends on the top of your list today.

                              ◊

I will make time for my friends.

_____

_____

_____

_____

_____

April 25

HAPPINESS

Happiness is not a matter of intensity but of balance and order and rhythm and harmony.

Thomas Merton

◊

We all get into ruts. The ruts blind us to new options and challenges. Then we wonder why we are unhappy.

Balance is lacking in our lives. We need to balance quiet activities with active ones, intellectual activities with frivolous ones, selfish activities with giving ones. In fact, you could say every day of parenting is a balancing act.

It takes us a long time to learn how to look happiness in the face, to accept it when it comes our way. Out of chaos has come rhythm, order and harmony with mankind.

◊

I will add balance to my life.

_____

_____

_____

_____

_____

April 26

FEELINGS

I wanted to be the Loretta Young, Irene Dunne version of the perfect mother . . . I tried never to let the kids even see me cry.
Carol Burnett

◊

We seek perfection. Like the stars of movie classics, we think we must rise to all parenting occasions with aplomb. Close-up shot. Orchestra swells. Camera fades.

So we hide our true feelings from our children and even ourselves. Who are we kidding? Stuffing our feelings hurts us and our children. The kids begin to think of us as mechanical people and we do, too—running our lives on automatic.

Our children need to know we are ordinary people, vulnerable and scared like everyone else. Sharing our true feelings with children gives them permission to share their true feelings with us. Feelings make us who we are.

◊

I will let my children see my true feelings.

_____

_____

_____

_____

_____

April 27

RISKING

Success sometimes depends more on the will to leap, than on weighing the pitfalls and dangers of failure.

Dr. David Viscott

◊

We are scared. The risks of life, our goals, our jobs, our finances, our children are scary to us. Just when things look calm life sends us another zinger.

Life forces us to respond and some of our responses involve risk-taking. So we calculate, weigh the odds, and take a gamble on ourselves. Taking risks is a way of saying yes to life. Our children watch the process and store the information for future use.

Hidden in the deepest recesses of their minds is a message: My parents are willing to take risks and I am, too.

◊

I will encourage my kids to take intelligent risks.

_____

_____

_____

_____

_____

April 28

KINDNESS

Maybe we could be a little nicer to each other, more thoughtful, perhaps?

Robert Conklin

◊

When the temperature soared to 100 degrees, I placed a large pan of water in the back yard.

"Why is that pan by the bird feeder?" my daughter asked.

"It's water for the animals and birds," I said. "They need extra water in this heat."

"Oh, mom," my daughter said, sniffing a little, "that's so sweet it makes me cry."

My daughter and I learned something about kindness that day and loved each other more because of it. Our children need to know kindness dwells within us.

◊

I will treat my children and their animals with kindness.

_____

_____

_____

_____

_____

April 29

PRIORITIES

How many children die every day from some contagious disease, that would be living if we exercised the same vigilance over a child that we do over a cow?

Will Rogers

◊

Anyone who reads the newspapers knows children are at risk around the globe. In a moral sense, we are not merely parents to our own children, we are parents to all children. Children need our help as never before.

One parent cannot change the world. But we can work with other parents to affect positive change. Volunteering an hour a week, as a scout leader, religious education teacher or school mentor can change the lives of children.

Children are our hope for the future. Giving to children comes back to us a thousandfold.

◊

I will make children my top priority.

_____

_____

_____

_____

_____

April 30

INDEPENDENCE

In the last hazardous tunnel to adulthood, when teenage kids tug and pull their way to separation, it's easy to forget ... our children wish us well.

Ellen Goodman

◊

Teenage separation is hard on all members of the family. Our children's separation anxiety takes many forms, from introverted behavior, to noisy confrontation, to overt hostility.

Often we respond defensively to this kind of behavior. We assign bad feelings to our children. This knee-jerk response makes teenage separation, a necessary step on the path to adulthood, even more difficult. We forget our children have deep feelings for us and wish us well.

This is a time for total honesty. We need to tell our children we will miss them and always love them.

◊

I will credit my children with good feelings.

_____

_____

_____

_____

_____

May 1

RENEWAL

There is something renewing about a small child.
                                    Coretta Scott King

◊

Because we are adults, some of us think our responses are superior to children's responses. Untrue. Our kids do surprising and loving things every day.

I remember the day my two-year-old daughter gave me her first gift. Dressed in a denim sunsuit and sunbonnet, my daughter toddled along until she spotted a dandelion growing in the crack of the sidewalk. She stooped down and carefully picked the flower.

"Mommy!" she said, hugging my leg and thrusting the dandelion into my hand.

My daughter's one-word greeting was filled with love. To this day, every time I see children picking dandelions, my eyes fill with tears.

◊

I will find renewal in my children.

_____

_____

_____

_____

_____

May 2

IDENTITY

All in all, they (children) are the joy of my life. I will not let my life be engrossed entirely in them and I struggle to keep my own freedom.

Pearl Buck

◊

Can we be good parents and maintain successful careers? The "career vs. children dilemma" makes us feel as if we have joined a tug–of–war.

Happy as we are about being parents, we still have to work at retaining our own identities. The tug–of–war becomes more intense as children grow older. Some days we cannot even think. Clearly, we must find ways to retain a sense of self.

As we become more experienced, we discover parenting does not eclipse our identities, it enhances them.

◊

I will strive to retain my identity.

_____

_____

_____

_____

_____

May 3

ROLES

For all of the child's teachers the first and most enduring ones are parents.

William H. Hooks

◊

We are our children's first teachers. Parents teach children important things: their first words, the difference between hot and cold, right and wrong. Our children remember what we have taught them.

A curious child wants answers immediately. We need to seize the moment when it comes to teaching. The casual interests of a pre-schooler could turn into a vocation. Learning may be reinforced with trips, books and craft projects.

The time we spend teaching children is always time well spent.

◊

I will take the time to be parent and teacher.

_____

_____

_____

_____

_____

May 4

GIVING

Everything I've done amounts to nothing unless we can make a difference for the children.

Dr. Karl Menninger

◊

Is something missing from your life? Perhaps you are missing the most critical ingredient of all—giving.

Everything about life feels different when we give ourselves to children. Our gifts do not have to come in be-ribboned packages. The time we share, the listening we do, the understanding we display and the laughter we release are long-lasting gifts our children will carry into the future.

The brilliant psychiatrist, Dr. Karl Menninger, understood the importance of giving. He felt his many accomplishments were nil unless he had done something to better children's lives. Children give purpose to our lives and make them meaningful.

◊

I will make each day count for children.

_____

_____

_____

_____

_____

May 5

GOALS

Once you have a child you stop thinking in terms of your lifespan only.

Pat Benatar

◊

Parenting changes our thinking. We become concerned about the survival of the giant redwoods, safe landfills and clean ground water. Will there be anything left for our children?

Saving the earth is more than talk, it is an absolute necessity. We must stop polluting the earth if our children are to live quality lives. The respect we have for the earth will be mirrored by our children. And our children's children.

We can make ecology one of our goals and work towards that goal with our children. Planet earth is worth saving—a true miracle.

◊

I will help my children care for planet earth.

_____

_____

_____

_____

_____

May 6

WISDOM

If you want something really exotic in the way of a conversation with a child, ask a philosophical question.

Barbara Walters

◊

Anyone who thinks they can fool children is a fool. Kids are savvy about life.

This is the perfect day to sit on a park bench and talk with our children. Patience will be rewarded. Before we know it, we will be discussing personalities, current events, and philosophy—to name just a few topics.

Our children are aware of life's problems and come up with some wacky solutions. Listen carefully, for a lot of our children's solutions have merit. You do not need to be old, to be wise.

◊

I will consider the wisdom of children.

_____

_____

_____

_____

_____

May 7

PLAY

We may not be sure what kind of play children need at different times . . . but fortunately children have a way of letting us know.

Fred Rogers and Barry Head

◊

Children's play must be the eighth wonder of the world. Without script or props, our children transform themselves into farmers, pilots, doctors, animals, parents and back to children again.

Our children play differently at different times in their lives. Preschoolers like role-playing, whereas teen-agers may prefer competitive sports. We need to be in sync with our children about their play, even if it is at the expense of time.

Watching children at play is watching the drama of life. A little play can save the day.

◊

I will value children's play.

_____

_____

_____

_____

_____

May 8

NUTRITION

How many days can a child eat chicken without beginning to squawk?

Phyllis Naylor

◊

When we serve our children leftovers three nights in a row they complain.

We are not mind readers. Our kids need to tell us which meals they liked and which they did not. Allowing our children to give us input makes them feel important. Their opinions really do count.

Although our children may help us with shopping, basic nutrition is our responsibility. We love our children enough to feed them healthy meals, including leftovers.

◊

I will feed my children healthy meals.

_____

_____

_____

_____

_____

May 9

QUIET

What is this life if, full of care, we have no time to stand and stare.

W. H. Davies

◊

Words can be intrusive. No words are necessary when we see a deer standing in the woods, watching us with dark eyes and looking ready to bolt. The beauty of the moment speaks for itself.

Today's children are bombarded by words from radio, television, boom boxes, headsets and sometimes all at once. This cacophony of sound constitutes noise pollution. Children need time in their lives to simply stand and stare.

We can help our children develop their other senses, taste, touch, smell, balance and sight. Take hold of your children's hands and stare at life. Our mental snapshots are worth billions of words.

◊

I will take the time to stand and stare.

_____

_____

_____

_____

_____

May 10

RESPECT

Anger begets anger; respect begets respect.

Attributed to *Joseph Stoll*

◊

Respect is nothing more than the willingness to show caring for others. Our children learn respect from us. It is possible to disagree with our children and still respect them.

Do not assume your kids know this. The lesson may have to be spelled out, stated in a short sentence such as, "I disagree with you but respect your right to an opinion." Depending on the situation, you might wish to explain your reasoning.

In time, our children learn that respect and love are two sides of the same coin. Because we respect them, they respect us.

◊

I will respect my children.

_____

_____

_____

_____

_____

May 11

DISCIPLINE

Parents owe their children consistency in discipline and firm guidelines.

Ann Landers

◊

When we are inconsistent about discipline, kids don't know what to expect. We think and talk about discipline, but do we look at ourselves? How often has our discipline been inconsistent? Did we take the time to think things through?

Inconsistent discipline confuses kids and makes them feel as if they are playing a game without knowing the rules. So, put the rules in writing and post them on the refrigerator door. Now everybody knows what to expect, including us.

Surprising as it sounds, children are actually looking for discipline from us. Consistent discipline is another way of saying "I love you."

◊

I will be consistent with discipline.

_____

_____

_____

_____

_____

May 12

STRESS

I don't know how I ever managed to make it through the week.

Peg Bracken

◊

There is no vacation from parenting. Whether we are having an easy week or a stressful week, the demands of parenting persist. Some days we wonder if we are going to make it to supper, let alone the next day.

Stressful feelings are transmitted to our children. They may start acting agitated and we feel even worse. Our children benefit from seeing us face life in a rational manner. It is a waste of time to worry about the future. Worrying today will not stop something from happening tomorrow.

Taking one day at a time helps us to deal with stress.

◊

I will take parenting one day at a time.

_____

_____

_____

_____

_____

May 13

FAMILY

The story (of parenting) goes on; it is unlike any other I have ever been a part of, and it goes on.

                                                    Bob Greene

◊

Although the current parenting chapters are unique to us, they are also similar to previous chapters. Generations of family members have tried to make life better for their children.

Parenting is a continuum. Placing ourselves on this continuum helps us to feel connected with grandparents and great-grandparents. And documenting our family history on video or audio tapes, in journals, and with artifacts helps our children to do the same.

Some day this historical evidence will help our children with parenting. The parenting adventure goes on.

◊

I will think of parenting as an ongoing adventure.

_____

_____

_____

_____

_____

May 14

PAIN

It is at the moment when we are moved to see and ease their pain that we realize the best that is within us.

Jim Klobuchar

◊

Nothing is worse than a child in pain. Physical pain, such as a broken leg, may be relieved by medical treatment. Psychiatric pain, such as the pain of depression, is more difficult to treat. Each type of pain deserves our full attention.

As hard as we try, parents cannot immunize their children against pain. Children learn how to handle pain by feeling and confronting it. However, we can listen to our children, commiserate with them, give endless hugs and connect them with suitable treatment.

Helping to ease a child's pain brings out the best that is within us. All of us learn ways of coping.

◊

I will help my children cope with pain.

_____

_____

_____

_____

_____

May 15

OPENNESS

Somewhere in us today there lives that solo pilot, that African explorer, that navigator of uncharted seas.

Judith Viorst

◊

Lethargy creeps up on us slowly, like a cool wind on a spring night. It is easier to stay at home and watch television than to go out.

Just because we are parents does not mean we cannot be adventurers. There is an adventurer inside each of us. We are more than fuddy–duddy parents, we are exciting people, open to new ideas and experiences. Our adventures are more exciting when they include children.

Our children will be open to change because we—the adventurers—have shown them how.

◊

I will remain open to new experiences.

_____

_____

_____

_____

_____

May 16

LETTING GO

As parents master the difficult task of letting go, they open the door for their adult child's friendship and love.

                              Jean Okimoto and Phyllis Stengal
                                        ◊

None of us learned to ride a two–wheeler instantly. Learning how to balance on a bike took lots of practice. Similarly, letting go of our children takes lots of practice.

Today is a good day to start letting go. We can squelch our fears and let our kids do something new. Letting go takes many forms: car privileges, part–time employment, travel, etc.

As we let go of our children, they begin to perceive us differently. We are no longer moms and dads, we are friends and confidants. The funny thing about letting go is that it enables our kids to boomerang back.

                                        ◊

I will consciously work at letting go.

_____

_____

_____

_____

_____

May 17

HAPPINESS

The heart can be filled up anywhere on earth.
                                        Bill Holm
◊

Want to learn more about your children? Ask them what makes them happy.

Teenagers may tell stories about their friends. While friends add to our children's happiness, be on the look-out for kids who depend on others for happiness. These kids wait for their friends to make plans, mimic emotions and go along with the crowd, no matter what the consequences.

In time, our children discover true happiness comes from within. Their hearts may be filled up anywhere on earth. We cannot be happy for our children. They must figure that out for themselves.
◊

I will help my children figure out what makes them happy.

_____

_____

_____

_____

_____

May 18

TIME

Think of the time you spend with your child as an investment in a sort of sacred savings account.
                    Linda Albert and Michael Popkin
                              ◊

Many is the teacher who would turn down a salary raise in return for extra time. And many is the parent who feels the same way. Time is an increasingly precious commodity.

Spending a few minutes with our children is a way of showing love. A few minutes can be as valuable as a few hours. Caring time makes a difference in our children's lives. Regular deposits of caring time add up with the sureness of pennies in a piggy bank.

Of all the memories of childhood, our kids will remember most the time we spent with them.
                              ◊

I will make time for my children.

_____

_____

_____

_____

_____

May 19

COMPETITION

One of the greatest mistakes that can be made by a man of my age is to get involved in athletic competition with children—unless of course, they are under six.

Bill Cosby

◊

Competing with our children is a fool's errand. A clear boundary separates parents from children and that boundary is age. No matter what we do or how we look, we are the parents and our children are the offspring. This fact will never change.

We do not have to exhibit regressive behavior and dress like teenagers in order to feel young. Youthful memories and ideas and goals will always connect us with our children. Our role is clear—act like mature parents and age with dignity.

◊

I will resist competing with my children.

_____

_____

_____

_____

_____

May 20

LOVE

Love whispers to your heart in many ways.
                                                    Barry Ellsworth

◊

Sometimes our children's expressions of love do not look like what they are.

My daughter expressed her love for me in an unusual way. Her first grade class was engrossed in a reading activity that involved cutting pictures from magazines. Instead of cutting out pictures, my daughter cut out discount coupons. When she came home from school, she raced towards me, a fistful of coupons in her hand. "Here!" she said happily. "These are for you."

This simple expression of love still whispers to my heart.

◊

I will accept unusual expressions of love.

_____
_____
_____
_____
_____

May 21

STRESS

In these transitional and stressful times, it is particularly important that we try to look at the world the way in which hurried children do.

David Elkind

◊

Do children feel stress? Countless articles have documented the existence of childhood stress and its causes.

We live in a fast–paced world and the pace is accelerating. This acceleration affects our children. If we feel pressured, think of how our children feel, rushing to school, participating in extracurricular activities, taking lessons, keeping up with homework and dealing with the daily news.

Mentally reversing roles with children helps us to understand them. We can look at the world through the eyes of our hurried children. And we can slow down.

◊

I will be alert to signs of stress in my children.

_____

_____

_____

_____

_____

May 22

I expect my children to be like me, only better.
                              Angela Barron McBride

◊

    The expectations we have for our children border on fantasy. We want our children to be like us and unlike us at the same time.

    Our expectations make us confuse physical likenesses with mental likenesses. We cannot force our children to think like we do. They are separate individuals with minds of their own. Neither education, nor experience, nor parenting will change this.

    We can accept our children's differences. Acceptance comes when we identify our feelings, find ways of coping and move on with life. And we can have reasonable expectations for our children.

◊

I will have reasonable expectations for my children.

_____

_____

_____

_____

_____

May 23

INTELLIGENCE

The mind, which sometimes presumes to believe that there is no such thing as a miracle, is itself a miracle.

M. Scott Peck, M.D.

◊

Children's minds are capable of inventing things far beyond adult imaginations. So museums and non-profit groups have sponsored exhibits and contests for child inventors. The results are wondrous, everything from a floating puzzle for the bathtub to a toilet paper roll that tells when the paper is almost out.

Some children prefer to draw their inventions. Children's drawings of machines are replete with intelligence and humor. Long explanations of how the machines work usually accompany the drawings.

If you have ever doubted the existence of miracles, doubt no more. Our children's minds are true miracles. Let us foster their intellectual development.

◊

I will foster my children's intellectual development.

_____

_____

_____

_____

_____

May 24

HEALTH/SPORTS

I want you to do well in your sports, and I want even more to have you do well with your books; but I do not expect you to stand first in either, if so to stand could cause you overwork and hurt your health.

Theodore Roosevelt

◊

This touching letter from President Roosevelt to his son began with the words, "Blessed Ted". The salutation says something about the man who wrote it. Like all parents, President Roosevelt wanted his son to succeed, but not if success robbed him of his health.

We need to guard our children's health carefully. Our vigilance includes food, rest, exercise, immunization, hygiene, recreation and well–being. Good health helps our children to do their best.

◊

I will watch over my children's health.

_____

_____

_____

_____

_____

May 25

NEEDS

Surely we have some rights in talking with our children about our needs.

Sharon Strassfeld and Kathy Green

◊

Children need to understand our needs if they are going to understand us.

Many of us are so used to being in charge, we do not want to admit our needs. To admit needs is to be vulnerable. We consider accepting help from our children equal to taking something from them.

If our children are going to have the courage to admit their needs, they must see us accepting ours. Admitting our needs to children is an act of love.

◊

I will admit my needs to children.

_____

_____

_____

_____

_____

May 26

FAMILY

At the end of your life, you will never regret not having passed one more test, not winning one more verdict or not closing one more deal. You will regret time not spent with a child, a friend or parent.

Barbara Bush

◊

Children give purpose to our lives. At the end of our days all that matters is family.

Family is all there is—the pinnacle. Yet the modern family is becoming an endangered species. Members of the extended family are scattered about like wind–borne leaves. Letters and long–distance phone calls are poor substitutes for personal contact.

We must take conscious steps to preserve the family unit, inviting grandparents for dinner, planning a cousin's party, or gathering the gang together for a reunion. We are a family!

◊

I will help my children get to know the members of the extended family.

_____

_____

_____

_____

_____

May 27

HAPPINESS

Dear God, please take your fingertips and lift the corners of my mouth at the beginning of each day.

Pearl Bailey

◊

The year my husband was stationed in Vietnam, I remained in Houston, Texas with my daughters. To keep myself occupied, I accepted a part–time teaching job.

My children attended the same school. En route, we made up a song which we called "Put Your Smile On With Rubber Bands." As the months passed the song became longer. We sang about putting our smiles on with school glue and sticky tape and bubble gum.

Many mornings I felt like crying. Singing that ridiculous song with my daughters made me smile and count my blessings.

◊

I will smile today.

_____

_____

_____

_____

_____

May 28

GENETICS

The baby is just a month old but she even has exactly my facial expression, my whole physiognomy, up to wrinkles on the forehead, and she lies there just as if she were composing a novel!
Fydor Dostoyevsky

◊

How miraculous it is to see replications—the family nose, the large brown eyes—in our children. Dostoyevsky was so pleased with his newborn daughter's resemblance to him, he credited her with his talents.

Genetic likenesses underscore our sense of family. We see likenesses to our children in old family snapshots. Just looking at our children brings us joy. Although we will see only a generation, or two of the 'children of the future', we do know they will look like family.

◊

I will find joy in physical similarities.

_____

_____

_____

_____

_____

May 29

CHILDCARE

All day I did the little things, the little things that do not show.

Blanche Bane Kuder

◊

Parents do hundreds of things that never show, like putting clean laundry away, baking chocolate chip cookies and buying materials for a school project. The satisfaction we receive from completing these tasks is minimal.

Leaving the tasks undone would certainly show. Our kids would be wearing grungy clothes, eating less nutritious snacks and slapping school projects together. Things would be makeshift at best.

Children need to see adults taking the time to do little jobs well. Little things have a way of adding up to big things. The pride we feel as parents stems partly from doing little jobs well.

◊

I will do little jobs well.

_____

_____

_____

_____

_____

May 30

DISCIPLINE

The child sees that his disobedience makes his parents angry, whereas it should make them sorrowful. Let your child know that his misdeeds sadden your heart, but never anger you.
Anonymous

◊

Getting angry about a child's misbehavior makes us feel better temporarily. Most of the time, however, anger is a wasted and non–productive emotion. Our kids simply get angry back at us.

Letting children know their behavior saddens our hearts is an alternate form of discipline. Our sadness is a sign of deep love and caring. The kids may disagree with our feelings but they cannot question their validity. Our feelings belong to us—we own them.

We cannot give up on our children when they do things that make us sorrowful. Good things happen when the heart speaks first.

◊

I will tell my children when misdeeds sadden my heart.

_____

_____

_____

_____

_____

May 31

THINKING

We, as parents, must give up our professed right to fix our children's thinking.

Dr. Charles H. Mayo

◊

Our children's "stinking thinking" throws us into a tizzy. We cannot pour logical thinking into a child's mind the same way we pour milk into a glass. Thinking is a product of intelligence, brain chemistry, life experience and the consequences of that experience.

If we cannot fix our children's "stinking thinking", we can let them suffer the immediate and long–term consequences of their behavior. Resist the temptation to fix your children's "stinking thinking" and let reality run its course.

◊

I will resist the temptation to fix my children's "stinking thinking."

_____

_____

_____

_____

_____

June 1

SEASONS

June brings tulips, lilies, roses. Fills the children's hands with posies.

Sara Coleridge

◊

Springtime ebbs and summertime appears. Our children give the season newfound meaning.

We hear summer in children's laughter, rattling bike fenders, bats hitting balls. We see summer in dandelion bouquets, lumpy backyard tents, popsicle mouths. We smell summer in grilling hot dogs, wet bathing suits, little sweating bodies. These smells, sights and sounds bring back memories.

Oh, to be a child again! We know time cannot be reversed. Still, we may find happiness in youthful memories and enjoying summer with our children.

◊

I will enjoy the changing seasons with my children.

_____

_____

_____

_____

_____

June 2

TALENT

You are unique. In the whole world there is only you. There is only one person with your talents, your experiences, your gifts.

Anonymous

◊

Children's talents are as diverse as any adults' talents. A child does not need to be a budding Picasso in order to develop his or her talent. Small talents comfort and sustain our children throughout their life.

We can nurture our children's talents in many ways: buying supplies, giving them a place to work, locating reference books for them. Although our children's talents are different than ours, we can still foster their development.

Being a mentor is a special talent of its own.

◊

I will foster my children's talents.

_____

_____

_____

_____

_____

June 3

COMPLAINING

I never knew her to utter a word of regret concerning our altered circumstances (poverty), nor did I ever know her children to do the like. For she had taught them and they drew their fortitude from her.

Mark Twain

◊

The diaries of Mark Twain tell the story of a talented man who often looked poverty in the face. Mark Twain credits his wife for her understanding, inner strength and the example she set for their children.

Constant complaining sets us up for unhappiness. Complaining does not provoke change, action does, so we might as well stop. When we complain we even sound boring to ourselves.

Our children need to see us working on solutions, drawing upon inner reserves, and maintaining a positive attitude about life. Years from now they will remember how we coped and draw strength from it.

◊

I will keep complaints to a minimum.

_____

_____

_____

_____

_____

June 4

ANGER

The family is one of the few settings where anger can be expressed.

Jerome Kagan

◊

Home is supposed to be a safe place to express anger. The family members are more apt to understand anger and its source. Not all children learn to express their anger at home, however.

Parents who have trouble expressing their anger usually have kids who have trouble expressing their anger. The children grow up thinking expressions of anger are taboo. These parents and children need to confront the anger within them and find suitable ways of expressing it.

Anger is a natural part of human personality and can have positive outcomes.

◊

I will help my children learn how to express anger.

_____

_____

_____

_____

_____

June 5

INDEPENDENCE

I was well enough to let my children run their own lives.
                                                          Betty Ford

◊

We have lots of control over young children and rightly so. Their health and safety depends upon us. The problem with control is that it is hard to give up.

Control can become a way of life, and can even become addictive in some cases. We have to be well enough to relinquish control. Our children will tell us and show us when this time has come.

Relinquishing control does not mean we have given up on parenting. Rather, it is an indication of good parenting. Our kids are maturing, accepting responsibility, and learning how to live independent lives. Hooray!

◊

I will foster independence in my children.

_____

_____

_____

_____

_____

June 6

STABILITY

I do try to keep things on an even keel for my children. But, God, it isn't always so easy.

Jaclyn Smith

◊

Many challenges come to parents. One of the most difficult challenges is maintaining a normal home life while our personal lives are in turmoil.

Even when our problems look insurmountable, we need to try and keep things on an even keel. Things need to proceed normally, with regular activities, mealtimes, and bedtimes. Children, especially very young children, will derive comfort from the routine itself.

Providing stability for our children is not easy. All we can do is try.

◊

I will try to keep things on an even keel.

_____

_____

_____

_____

_____

June 7

AUTONOMY

Your children are not your children. They are the sons and daughters of Life's longing for itself.

Kahlil Gibran

◊

Do you define yourself by your children? Some of us use our children as substitutes for goals we failed to achieve. The mother who wanted a singing career may push her tone–deaf daughter into taking voice lessons. The father who wanted to be a professional athlete may push his gentle son into competitive sports.

While our children belong to us biologically, they belong to life more, they are the sons and daughters of life itself. Autonomy is our children's destiny.

◊

I will encourage my children's autonomy.

_____

_____

_____

_____

_____

June 8

SPIRITUALITY

The truth we seek as parents—and as people in any kind of loving relationship—lies within each of us.
                    Jordan Paul, Ph.D. and Margaret Paul, Ph.D.
◊

When it comes to washing jeans, cooking spaghetti and wiping runny noses, we are right there. We are childcare experts. But many of us ignore spiritual care. In the back of our minds, we hope spirituality will take care of itself.

That does not stop us from asking questions. The answers to life's questions are not distant, they are close at hand, hidden deep inside us. Meditation helps us to know ourselves, develop spirituality and cope with crisis. Our children sense we are spiritual people, humbled by the beauty and wonder of life.

In seeking answers we are not questioning spirituality, we are confirming it.
◊

I will find comfort in spirituality.

June 9

LOVE

If we are moved by a loving act it will be because it exposes us not just to being loved, but to awe at the concept of love.

Willard Gaylin

◊

We are obsessed with data. Random surveys, phone surveys, questionnaires and statistical analyses are dumped into data bases. Sometimes we analyze things to death.

Love can be analyzed to death. So much time is spent on the analysis we become numb to love itself. We do not need to analyze love in order to feel it. Artists, poets, and musicians have tried to explain love for centuries and will probably be trying to explain it centuries from now.

Love simply is, an emotion worthy of awe. Let us spend our time cherishing love and those who love us.

◊

I will cherish love and not try to explain it.

_____

_____

_____

_____

_____

June 10

FORGIVENESS

Forgiveness works even when we get it only half right.
Eugene Kennedy

◊

Our children hurt us. Images of their behavior, like hateful words and physical aggression, remain with us forever. We remember things we wish we could forget.

Although we cannot banish all painful memories, we can take conscious steps to forgive our children. Similarly, our children can take conscious steps to forgive us. If we do not do this, we are condemning ourselves to mutual unhappiness.

We forgive our children because we love them. In forgiving, we open our hearts to peace.

◊

I will find the courage to forgive my children.

_____

_____

_____

_____

_____

June 11

CHANGE

Change is a form of hope.

Linda Ellerbee

◊

Whether it's alcohol, drugs, or compulsive gambling, addiction changes children. The drastic changes in our children's behavior scare us to the marrow of our bones. We wonder if our children have been changed forever.

While change symbolizes the unknown, it also symbolizes hope. With the right treatment and an after-care program, we hope our children will be able to turn their lives around. We hope they will change back into the loving children we knew.

◊

I will remember that change holds the promise of hope.

_____

_____

_____

_____

_____

June 12

EXPERIENCE

It is imperative that every child be able to face his own experience.

Viktor Lowenfeld

◊

Surprising as it sounds, there are kindergartners who come to school the first day never having used crayons, scissors or paste. Their parents were afraid the kids would get dirty, or worse, dirty up the house.

Kids thrive on creative experiences. These experiences help our children to improve eye–hand coordination and give them a chance to express their thoughts.

So many good things in life, like eating chocolate cake and playing in the sand box, are messy. That is precisely what makes them so much fun. Kids and messes go together like peanut butter and jelly.

◊

I will let my children enjoy messy experiences.

June 13

ACCEPTANCE

Accept parenthood as a series of tradeoffs.
                    Roberta Plutznik and Maria Laghi
                              ◊

It does not take us long to figure out parenting involves tradeoffs. We trade vocabulary development with a two-year-old's penchant for saying "no" a hundred times a day. We trade loaning the car to adolescents with taking the time to drive them to the football game.

Every tradeoff makes us feel edgy. Our parental control is slipping away. Will the kids slip away from us too?

We must accept the fact that tradeoffs come with the territory. Tradeoffs demonstrate our willingness to negotiate with children. Our children discover we are not their enemies, but loving parents who trust them.
                              ◊

I will accept parenting as a series of tradeoffs.

_____

_____

_____

_____

_____

June 14

ATTITUDE

We should take what joy we can together, given the brevity of our lives and the amount of grief there is in the world.
Herbert Kohl

◊

All of us know grouches, people who put a damper on happiness wherever they go. If we let them, these grouches will spoil the happiest of occasions.

We need to be able to pull positive attitudes out of our pockets when the need arises. Balance is important here. Depressing stories can be balanced with humor. Complaints can be balanced with compliments.

The difference between enduring life and savoring it is often a positive attitude. Get out your butterfly net. You'll want to catch the smiles, laughter and joy when they zigzag by.

◊

I will welcome joy when it comes my way.

_____

_____

_____

_____

_____

June 15

ARGUING

Am I acting or reacting?

Charlie Shedd

◊

Arguing with our children gets us right where it hurts. We shout back at our kids without thinking. The knee–jerk response undermines the trust between parents and children. Trust sinks with the swiftness of a stone.

There is merit to the axiom about counting to three before we speak. Before we lash out at our children, we need to ask ourselves three questions. Am I acting? Am I reacting? Am I over–reacting?

The answers to these questions determine how we talk to our kids. It is hard for us to be mature in the middle of an argument. However, we can monitor ourselves and guard against over–reacting. Then too, we always have the right to remain silent.

◊

I will guard against over–reacting.

_____

_____

_____

_____

_____

June 16

BLAME

It has often been said, that in becoming parents our-selves, we now understand what our mother and father went through and thus can no longer blame and denounce them.

Judith Viorst

◊

How easily we blame our parents for our problems. Childhood experiences affect our current behavior, but they cannot rob us of the power of choice. We may choose between living in the past or living in the present.

Today is the perfect day to discard emotional baggage. Our children need us now. Why waste time dwelling on the past? Why waste time worrying about the future? Only by living in the present will we find happiness.

Adult parents still have to work at growing up. The first step is to stop blaming our parents for our mistakes. We have this day, this hour, this moment, to spend with our children.

◊

I will not blame my parents for my mistakes.

_____

_____

_____

_____

_____

June 17

CONNECTEDNESS

As the mother grows and the father grows, the children grow and the society grows, because we're all one piece.
                                        Angela Barron McBride

◊

Each of us is a piece of the humankind puzzle. Our parenting can affect the survival of human–beings. If people are to live in peace, they must learn to care about each other.

Parents are the connectors. There are many connections we can make. The connections we select depend upon the personalities and interests of our children. Our kids learn about different ways of living and that people are still much the same. All different— all alike—we walk the earth together.

It is normal for parents to want better lives for their children. Better lives begin with connections.

◊

I will help my child to feel connected with others.

_____

_____

_____

_____

_____

June 18

PETS

Almost every young child yearns to have a pet. The same, however, cannot always be said of parents.

Maria Piers and Genieve Landau

◊

For a time, my husband and I moved every 10 months. Moving this often was so tiring, we decided not to complicate our lives with pets.

At my daughter's new school, the teacher asked the class to describe family pets. My daughter talked about a tree frog that lived on a plant beside the front door. I felt like a failure when I heard the story. Other children had described dogs, cats, birds, fish and horses, whereas my daughter had described a non–existent pet.

We moved again. The first thing my husband and I did was get a puppy. All of us were enthralled with the dog and we have had a dog ever since, along with the usual array of hamsters and fish. Pets have taught my children a lot about caring.

◊

I will give my children the fun of caring for pets.

_____

_____

_____

_____

_____

June 19

CHILDHOOD

Childhood is a blissful time of play and fantasizing, of uninhibited sensual delight.

Clare Boothe Luce

◊

Children are part of the labor force. At this very moment, there are people foisting adult jobs on children. Newspapers run stories about child labor in industry and child labor at home.

The number of very young children who are caring for even younger siblings is rising sharply. Childhood seems to be a vanishing season. If we do nothing else, parents must give their children a chance to act like children.

Every child has the right to childhood. Children need to figure out how they fit into families, extended families and society in general. How else are they going to learn to be parents?

◊

I will ensure my children have a childhood.

_____

_____

_____

_____

_____

June 20

OPTIMISM

The optimism of finding happiness regardless of false starts or disastrous mistakes is what I hope I have given my children.

Ellen Walker

◊

For some of us, optimism is as distant and elusive as the pot of gold at the end of the rainbow. As the rain shower nurtures the flowers, so optimism nurtures our souls.

Kids need to see their parents feeling optimistic. We must rekindle the flame of optimism and keep it burning, if not for ourselves, than for our children. Life is dark and shadowed without optimism.

Despite false starts, failure to carry through and disastrous mistakes, we must try to be optimistic. An optimistic attitude can turn dark clouds into rainbows.

◊

I will try to be optimistic about life.

June 21

ADOPTION

Gracie picked out Ronnie (for adoption) because he needed her most.

George Burns

◊

Adoptive parents are blessed. The unforeseen circumstances of life have placed children in our care. Certainly our adopted children need us, but we need them, also.

Parenting is a noble calling. It asks the best of us and makes us become the best we can be. Adopted children give purpose to our lives.

When we tell our children they are adopted, we will tell them they came to us because of love. We had so much love to share we wanted to share it with children. And we will tell them our love is unconditional. Love is not contingent upon genetics.

◊

I will love my children unconditionally.

_____

_____

_____

_____

_____

June 22

BEHAVIOR

Neither of us wanted bratty children.

Dr. Benjamin Spock

◊

Bratty. Saying the word conjures up images of screaming, hyperactive, manipulative children.

Allowing bratty behavior to go unchecked sets a dangerous precedent. Bratty kindergartners grow into bratty teenagers, and bratty teenagers grow into bratty adults. These are the folks who exhibit "ME—FIRST" behavior and walk over the psyches of colleagues with cleated shoes.

It is natural for children to test their parents. However, we need to set limits on this behavior. If you are worried about whether you are doing the right thing, remember, bratty children will probably bring bratty grandchildren home to visit. Oy!

◊

I will check bratty behavior when it starts.

_____

_____

_____

_____

_____

June 23

PERSONALITY

Train up a child in the way he should go; and when he is old, he will not depart from it.

Holy Bible, Proverbs 22: 6

◊

Parenting is chancy. The chances are good, however, that the child who learns to share in kindergarten will become a staunch community volunteer.

Imprints of childhood remain with us throughout life. We need to imprint our children with the basic skills: how to take turns, how to play fairly, how to say please and thank you, how to take care of themselves, how to clean up a mess, how to do a good deed.

Hopefully, when our children are grown, they will not depart from this behavior. We will take the time to train our children in the ways they should go.

◊

I will train my child for the future.

_____

_____

_____

_____

_____

June 24

CHORES

I have learned that my kids, like most kids, would rather work all night long in a salt mine than rake leaves at home.

Phil Donahue

◊

Contrary to popular opinion, there is nothing wrong with hard work. Our children get satisfaction from doing a job well. Asking them to help with chores is a way of teaching them responsibility.

Close your ears to your kid's stories about friends and how their parents "don't make them do anything." Because we want our children to be self–sufficient when they leave our care, we ask them to help.

We need not feel guilty about asking our children to help us. Three year–olds may help by putting their toys away. In time, our children learn that helping is fun and they enjoy being part of the family team. Job satisfaction starts early in life.

◊

I will ask my children to help with chores.

_____

_____

_____

_____

_____

June 25

COURAGE

Only when parents and teachers are encouraging does a child develop courage.

Dr. Rudolf Dreikurs and Pearl Cassel

◊

Webster's dictionary defines courage as the ability to face danger without fear. The dictionary does not say that courage develops slowly, with small successes over time. Parents and teachers help children to develop courage.

A parent, holding fast to the rear wheel and shouting encouraging words, helps a child learn to ride a two–wheeler. A teacher, holding fast to goals and offering encouraging words, helps a child learn to read. Our children's small successes add up to courage.

There are times, in the course of parenting, when parents need a special kind of courage in order to persist, to keep on keeping on. We find that courage because we love our children.

◊

I will help my children to develop courage.

_____

_____

_____

_____

_____

June 26

CHILDCARE

How can a job as important as childcare be so undervalued?
Louise De Grave

◊

How do we solve the childcare dilemma? Husbands may switch roles with their wives, or a family member may care for relatives' children. Some of us become daycare providers.

Childcare workers are undervalued in our society. Many people think childcare is unimportant work that demands little intelligence. Appallingly low wages reinforce this myth.

Investing in quality childcare is an investment in the future. Well–adjusted children will probably grow into well–adjusted adults. Taking care of children is the most important job in the world.

◊

I will look upon childcare as the most important job in the world.

_____

_____

_____

_____

_____

June 27

PEERS

Their (teenagers') reliance on parents for advice and support seems to grow less with each exchange on the phone
Leslie S. Kaplan Ed.D

◊

When teenagers are in the house the phone rings day and night. If the phone rings one more time, we are sure we will let out a primal scream.

Every phone call pushes the kids closer to their peers. Instead of turning to us, they turn to their peers for advice. Excessive use of the phone infringes upon the rights of other family members.

Setting limits on phone time is not unreasonable. The phone is primarily a communications tool, not a recreational tool and should be used as such. We would be wise to know who our children are calling. Peer influence is not the same as peer pressure.

◊

I will factor my children's peers into parenting.

_____

_____

_____

_____

_____

June 28

HUMOR

Children are becoming an endangered species, energy has reached crisis proportions, marriages are on the decline and the only ones having any fun any more are the research rats.

Erma Bombeck

◊

God bless humorists.

It is difficult to laugh, though, when we are confronted by angry, hostile, combative children. Laughter becomes dormant. Once laughter is dormant, it is hard to start again, as balky as a cold, un–driven car.

After my father died I lost my sense of humor. The grieving process, coupled with multiple crises, took away my humor completely. Nothing seemed funny. This was scary because I had always been known for my wacky sense of humor.

What could I do? I read humorous books, forced myself to attend social functions, and chose one special friend as a confidant. My sense of humor returned and I tend it regularly.

◊

I will maintain my sense of humor.

_____

_____

_____

_____

_____

June 29

SELF–CARE

Treating yourself right conveys the message that your happiness and fulfillment do not depend on anyone else's approval
Sonya Friedman, Ph.D.

◊

Learning how to take care of ourselves is one of the most difficult lessons of life.

Some parents who practice self–care suspect it is a vain and selfish pursuit. Actually, self–care is a symptom of a stable personality. We are mature enough to recognize the need for self–care. Practicing self–care sends a message to our children: We are worthy of self–care and do not rely on others for our happiness.

Self–care is worth the effort. We have the right to treat ourselves right.

◊

I will treat myself right.

_____

_____

_____

_____

_____

June 30

DISCIPLINE

Love is reason enough for the moment.

Sam Levenson

◊

Discipline can be a never–ending challenge. As our children mature, they question discipline, swearing, arguing, yelling and generally hoping to wear us down.

We find ourselves playing mind games. Our children's arguments are really diversionary tactics, designed to shift our attention away from their behavior. Many relationships have been destroyed or damaged by this technique.

Enforcing discipline takes lots of courage. We do not need to explain our reasoning to our children. Love is reason enough.

◊

I will discipline my children because I love them.

_____

_____

_____

_____

_____

July 1

WORKAHOLICS

Cutting back is certainly not all there is to growing happiness, but like clearing weeds and preparing soil, it is a critical first step.

Hugh Prather

◊

Workaholic parents are so pressed for time, they barely have time for their children. Cutting back on work seems impossible.

But our children want to make the most of every summer day, riding bikes, splashing in the pool, selling lemonade, planting zinnia seeds, blowing bubbles in the sunshine. Joining them in these activities is better for our health than surrendering to workaholic tendencies.

The children of workaholic parents are lonely people. We are lonely also and yearn for our children while we are at work. Before summer is gone, let us share these lazy, beautiful days with our children.

◊

I will combat my workaholic tendencies.

_____

_____

_____

_____

_____

July 2

MEMORIES

All grown-ups were once children—although few of them remember it.

Antoine De Saint–Exupery

◊

Few adults think about their childhood memories these days, or so it seems. We are so intent upon getting ahead, we do not bother to look back. Yet, recalling our childhood experiences can help us to be better parents.

Some memories are piercingly sad, while others have an iridescent beauty. Happy, sad or in between, our childhood memories put us in touch with our feelings. Being in touch with our feelings helps us to stay in touch with our kids.

Today is a good day to share some of our childhood memories with our children. We were not always stodgy adults. Once we were silly, impulsive, rollicking, messy, boisterous, carefree children and our kids need to know that about us.

◊

I will remember what it was like to be a child.

_____

_____

_____

_____

_____

July 3

SPIRITUALITY

You become a certain kind of person when you choose to believe that there is a pattern and purpose to the universe, when you learn to see the world through the eyes of faith.

Rabbi Harold Kushner

◊

Spiritual parents see the world through the eyes of faith. Belief in a Higher Power helps us to grow from tragedy and comforts us in times of sorrow. Life makes more sense.

Just as the world's religions developed over time, so our spirituality develops over time. The frantic pace of our lives can obscure spirituality. We suspect we have lost our faith, only to discover it was there all the time, ready and waiting to be reactivated.

Knowing we are spiritual people makes our children feel more secure. Our spirituality is not a sign of weakness, it is a sign of strength. Spirituality changes the way we live and touches the lives of those we meet.

◊

I will let my children know I am a spiritual person.

_____

_____

_____

_____

_____

July 4

ATTENTION

Children bask in the warmth of their family's undivided attention like sunbathers in the sun.

                            Linda Albert and Michael Popkin
◊

All of us need attention if we are to thrive. Children need our undivided attention.

Undivided attention is a mutual gift, a bonding between parents and children. We focus upon our children and they focus upon us. They watch our body language, verbal responses, attempts at humor, expressions of empathy.

Giving children undivided attention helps us to know them. Love deepens. Our children bask in the light of our attention because, to them, we are the sun.

◊

I will find time to give my children undivided attention.

_____

_____

_____

_____

_____

July 5

INTERESTS

Parents play a crucial role in influencing what students will find stimulating.

Raymond Wlodkowski and Judith Jaynes

◊

Parents play a crucial role, in some cases, an irreversible role, in shaping children's interests. That explains why some families are known for certain occupations. An artist's children, for example, may become artists or enter art–related fields.

We must use our influence wisely. Even when our children's interests are vastly different from ours, their interests deserve our support. This support must continue as our children's interests develop and change.

Childhood is a time of exploring interests. The personal interests of our children make each of them special and unique.

◊

I will take the time to show interest in my children's interests.

_____

_____

_____

_____

_____

July 6

MATURITY

Growing up...that's what being a child is all about and that's what being a parent is all about.

Angela Barron McBride

◊

We think we are mature parents until something happens and we start screaming like cartoon characters. How embarrassing.

Growing up is not confined to the young. As we grow older we continue the process of growing up. Growth is more meaningful if we grow along with our children. Some of the things our kids love about us are our child like qualities. These qualities are not something to be embarrassed about, but something to smile about, child–to–child connections, the glue that holds parents and kids together.

Spurts of silliness and playfulness make us real to our children. We are not always mature, polished, perfect people, we are growing, changing and evolving adults—in sync with our kids.

◊

I will grow up with my children.

_____

_____

_____

_____

_____

July 7

SELF-CARE

The only way to survive parenthood is to survive life.
                                                    Eda Le Shan

◊

The parent who extols the virtues of healthy food, a good night's sleep and regular exercise, may be the same parent who practices self-neglect.

We say that we don't have the time to take care of ourselves and our children come first. This is nothing more than rationalization. Are we less worthy of care than our children?

Taking care of ourselves ultimately makes us better equipped to be parents. If we are to survive parenthood, we have to survive life. Practicing self-care helps us to do that.

◊

I will take care of myself in order to survive.

_____

_____

_____

_____

_____

July 8

APPROVAL

If I'm not ruled by external approval, then my children won't be either, perhaps.

Jon Voight

◊

Approval can have far–reaching effects. The teen-agers who seek the approval of their peers can become clones of each other. A teenager's quest for approval may reflect our quest.

If we are not ruled by outside approval, our children will probably not be, either. They discover that their opinion of themselves is far more important than what others think of them.

We can help our children to seek their own approval by joining forces with them. With love and encouragement, our children learn they can be true to themselves. And we become truer to ourselves in the process.

◊

I will seek my own approval.

_____

_____

_____

_____

_____

July 9

TANTRUMS

Many a child is master of his parents through crying.
Anonymous

◊

A child in the midst of a tantrum—crying, scream-ing and thrashing about—is a sight to behold. Tantrums often occur when children are overtired. But some chil-dren use tantrums to manipulate their parents.

Too often children are rewarded for this behavior. Giving candy to a child in the throes of a tantrum sends a message: If you scream loud enough and long enough I will give in and give you a treat.

Teenagers can stage noisy and spectacular tan-trums. Despite escalating behavior, we can choose to be calm. Mindful of our children's needs we can tell them, with words and hugs, we love them, even when they are having tantrums.

◊

I will respond calmly to tantrums.

_____

_____

_____

_____

_____

July 10

PRAISE

If we praise them for everything they do they are going to start learning, doing things, just to please us, and the next step is that they are going to become worried about not pleasing us.

John Holt

◊

Excessive praise puts kids on guard and can have negative results. Our children mentally cancel out the praise and worry about pleasing us. Worry can get all out of proportion.

Praise does not need to be long or flowery. Short, specific praise works best. "I like the way the sun fills up the sky in your picture." "You're being a good friend when you pull a wagon full of kids." "You were kind to your baby brother today."

Children respond to genuine praise. What's more, they remember it. Have you praised your kids today?

◊

I will give my children genuine praise.

_____

_____

_____

_____

_____

July 11

MOTHERS

Every moment of the day is about mothering.
                                        Sally Field
◊

Mothering infuses the myriad of tasks which fill our days. No matter what we are doing, we are thinking about mothering.

The smallest things about mothering, like dirty clothes strewn all over the bedroom floor, can drive us nuts. Seeing the havoc makes us feel grouchy. Mothers need to separate childcare activities from actual mothering.

How we interact with our children is what is important. Did we listen? Did we encourage? Did we empathize? Did we show love? Time spent in mothering is not wasted. The valuable skills we develop as mothers may be applied to other facets of life.

◊

I will learn from mothering.

_____

_____

_____

_____

_____

July 12

PEER PRESSURE

Things go wrong because you're not the only one with your children all their lives. Once they get out in society amid peer-pressure...you pray, a lot.

Carol Burnett

◊

We worry about peer pressure. But we cannot be with our kids every moment of every day. All we can do is pray.

I was a young child during World War II and remember hearing songs in support of the war effort on the radio. One song was entitled, "Comin' In On A Wing And A Prayer." When my daughters became adolescents I recalled the title. I had never been the mother of teenagers before and, as pilots say, was flying by the seat of my pants, trusting my instincts, coming in on a wing and a prayer. Often I cried as I prayed.

My daughters are grown now, mature, responsible adults in charge of their own lives. I am happy to report we all landed safely.

◊

I will pray about parenting.

July 13

PARTNERSHIP

Sometimes he would overrule me and let the children do as they wanted, which made me furious. But we never quarreled in front of them.

Jehan Sadat

◊

Mothers and fathers do not always agree. Disagreeing with a mate makes us feel nervous, angry and queasy. Having a difference of opinion is one thing, but arguing in front of our children is another.

Children may misinterpret the quarrel and wrongly conclude their parents do not love each other anymore. Young children may feel especially anxious because they do not have large enough vocabularies to express their feelings.

Quarreling in front of our children should be avoided. It is better to work out differences behind the scenes, without an audience, and present a united front to our children. Parenting unites us.

◊

I will avoid quarreling in front of my children.

_____

_____

_____

_____

_____

July 14

SELF–HELP

The problem with books on discipline is that they never discuss the situations that come up at our house.

Phyllis Naylor

◊

Parenting books are popular these days. Many are vapid writing, too scholarly, packed with jargon or aimed at television sit–com families. We are looking for practical solutions to real–life problems.

Instead of turning to these books for comfort, we can turn to other parents. We can start a parents network or support group. Anecdotal accounts from other parents help us more than anything else. It is reassuring to know other parents have similar problems and feelings.

Why do we protect our alone–ness? Other parents are close by, ready and eager to help.

◊

I will seek help from other parents.

_____

_____

_____

_____

_____

July 15

LOVE

We must trust ourselves and love ourselves for the primary purpose of loving others.

Willard Gaylin

◊

How we feel about ourselves affects how we feel about others. Love for others begins with self–love, the ability to take care of ourselves, reward ourselves and commend ourselves. Self–love grows into the love of a mate, our children, members of the extended family and social groups.

When we love ourselves we are able to love others. With practice, we develop the ability to take "inner readings" and trust our parenting instincts. We have the power to listen to, and believe in ourselves. In some cases, our parenting instincts are more trustworthy than misleading facts.

◊

I will trust my parenting instincts.

_____

_____

_____

_____

_____

July 16

PROGRESS

*The small pains and disappointments keep us off our
mark a little.*

Tom Bodett

◊

Like potholes in the road, the disappointments
and pains of parenting keep us off our mark. We swerve in
our parenting instead of proceeding directly to our
destination.

Parents cannot react to every little thing. We need
to conserve our energy for the big things in life. When our
children are grown, it will not matter if they refused to eat
carrots or wore their hair in bizarre styles. Having happy,
well–adjusted and caring children is all that really matters.

The parenting road is filled with potholes. We
need to check our progress map from time to time to see
if we are on the right track.

◊

I will check my progress from time to time.

_____

_____

_____

_____

_____

July 17

HAPPINESS

The world's a very happy place, where every child should dance and sing.

Charles and Mary Lamb

◊

Life is filled with happiness, yet many of us do not experience it. We let our problems consume us. Consequently, we miss much of our children's dancing and singing.

Despite our helpless and hopeless feelings, our children have the right to dance and sing. Young children are pure, innocent and trusting. Their instinctive trust in life has much to teach us about coping. It seems as if our children are telling us to stop, look, listen and live.

This is a day to dance and sing with children, to celebrate the gift of life.

◊

I will celebrate life with my children.

_____

_____

_____

_____

_____

July 18

BEHAVIOR

A strong and healthy child has to be stubborn and defiant occasionally.

Herbert Kohl

◊

Defiance is hard enough to deal with, but twice as hard when our self–worth is challenged. We have been good parents. Why are our children so defiant?

The flip side of defiant behavior is apathy. Think of how we would feel if our kids were bland, predictable and totally dependent. We would feel terrible. Our children would be wind–up toys, not real people.

All children have times of stubbornness and defiance. We need to be calm, patient and empathetic. We also need to give our children unconditional love. Stubborn and defiant children grow into intelligent and rational adults. Amazing.

◊

I will view stubbornness and defiance as signs of a healthy personality.

_____

_____

_____

_____

_____

July 19

PLAY

When we treat our children's play as seriously as it deserves, we are helping them to feel the joy that's to be found.
                                        Fred Rogers and Barry Head
                                        ◊

Children's play is as hilarious as any comedy film. Seeing our kids dressed up in cast–off clothing, strutting around in oversize shoes and wearing floppy hats, sends us into gales of laughter.

Humorous as children's play appears, it is actually serious work. The way our children play, the length of play, the props they use and the talk that accompanies the play, tell us a lot about their thoughts. Children who role play about parenting are literally playing for their lives.

Treating children's play seriously makes them feel secure in their play and intensifies the happiness they get from it. In turn, our children learn to respect our play, however hilarious it may be.
                                        ◊

I will think of children's play as their work.

_____

_____

_____

_____

_____

July 20

INDEPENDENCE

One of the most valuable gifts we offer our adult children is the encouragement of autonomy.
                                    Jean Okimoto and Phyllis Stengall
◊

A child's desire for autonomy is hard on parents, a sort of push–pull experience. We push our children one day and pull them back the next. If we nurture our children's independence gently and continuously, everyone in the family will feel better.

Our children seek independence like flowers seek sunlight. Shielding them from the sunlight of autonomy stunts our children's personal growth. We may as well encourage our children's autonomy because they will achieve it anyway. Nature planned for our children to grow into autonomous adults.

◊

I will respect my children's need for independence.

_____

_____

_____

_____

_____

July 21

IMPORTANCE

Don't sell yourself short. You may never have proof of your importance, but you are more important than you think.
Robert Fulghum

Too bad we do not have proof of our importance, a printed receipt, engraved certificate, a shiny medal—something. At least visual proof would help us to believe in ourselves.

Parents and children are symbiotic personalities. Those of us who know ourselves, who are honest with our feelings and listen to our thoughts, know we are important. We are aware of what we have done for our children and what they have done for us.

Visual proof of our importance is unnecessary. We can value ourselves and the parenting we do.

◊

I will value myself and the parenting I do.

_____

_____

_____

_____

_____

July 22

REALITY

The parent needs to be a line both to reality and the child's inner self.

William H. Hooks

◊

The violence in our world is so rampant some days we do not want to read the newspaper. We waiver between telling our children the truth and protecting them from reality.

We are conduits for our children, a connection between the harsh realities of life and our children's inner selves. Avoiding power surges and outages, we concentrate on providing steady support.

Shielding our children from psychologically harmful events is not denial, it is good parenting. We want our children to know that we will care for them, protect them and always love them.

◊

I will serve as a conduit between the real world and my children's world.

_____

_____

_____

_____

_____

July 23

INFANTS

Certainly they (parents) can't change him into another kind of baby.

T. Berry Brazelton, M.D.

◊

It is impossible to change a nervous, colicky baby into a serene baby. While we affect our children in countless ways, we cannot transform them totally, and trying to do so is an exercise in futility.

The relentless desire to change our children blinds us to reality. We need to take the blinders off. Our children are not perfect and we are not perfect. In fact, some days our kids would gladly trade us in on newer, flashier models.

Our children are works in progress. When we love our children for who they are, and who they are not, life seems a lot happier. And more exciting, too. We can hardly wait to see the finished work.

◊

I will love my children for who they are.

_____

_____

_____

_____

_____

July 24

MESSINESS

The detritus from a two–year-old's getting her own chocolate ice cream from the freezer would drive some people berserk.

Alice Atkinson Lyndon

◊

Two–year–olds like to assert their independence. By allowing a two–year–old to make a peanut butter and jelly sandwich our kitchen can be totally trashed. We do not know whether to applaud or burst into tears. Sometimes we do both.

We must remember that messiness precedes orderliness. One cannot exist without the other. Our children learn to appreciate order after they have been distressed by messiness. In over–reacting to our children's messiness we only harm ourselves. Messes and messy kids can always be cleaned up.

◊

I will enjoy my children's messiness.

_____

_____

_____

_____

_____

July 25

WISDOM

I will not press wisdom on my children, it is not well to be too wise.

Pearl Buck

◊

Kids do not respond to parents who speak like oracles. That does not stop us from acting like talking heads. The desire to impart wisdom sounds like nagging to our children.

Many of us equate speech with power. As long as we are talking to our children, we think we have power over them. Our children will listen to us, believe us, take our advice and change their behavior. But the kids get fed up with our constant yammering and tune us out.

If we are so smart, why don't we credit our kids with smarts? Our children will derive more satisfaction from learning things on their own. Wise parents know when to shut up.

◊

I will try not to press wisdom on my children.

_____

_____

_____

_____

_____

July 26

RESPECT

We are not doing our children any favors by allowing them to "get away" with disrespect, especially towards us.

Peggy Finston, M.D.

◊

Letting children get away with disrespectful behavior sets them up for trouble.

Our disrespectful children grow into annoying adults who live their lives with total disregard for others. They don't realize their abrasive behavior repels others and puts them on the defensive. Disrespectful people are often lonely people. Who wants to spend time with a klutz?

We need to love our children enough to teach them respectful behavior—behavior that shows caring. We care about others so we say "please" and "thank you" and "I'm sorry." Our children learn these skills from us. Together, we can practice, practice, practice.

◊

I will teach my children to respect others.

_____

_____

_____

_____

_____

July 27

NURTURING

The devotion of a parent to a child—the combination of protecting them and pushing them out of the nest—is the epitome of leadership.

Alan Loy McGinnis

◊

Daily we adapt our parenting to our children's needs. Our nurturing gives children more than a sense of security, it gives them the chance to experiment. Because the results of nurturing are not immediately visible, many of us are plagued by self–doubt.

Nurturing affects our children's lives in ways we cannot foresee. Our intuitive nurturing is actually the epitome of leadership. While our children may not comment about nurturing, they are aware of it nevertheless.

The nurtured, secure children of today could grow up to be the nurturing, secure leaders of tomorrow.

◊

I will nurture my children in a variety of ways.

_____

_____

_____

_____

_____

July 28

PERFECTION

We cannot achieve perfection. Trying to do so will make us crazy.

Phyllis & David York and Ted Wachtel

◊

As we grow older, we become more aware of the tug of war between intellect and emotion. Our intellect warns us about striving for perfection, whereas our emotions push us toward the goal of perfection.

The desire for perfection can be so obsessive it harms parents and children alike. A mania for perfection is, itself, a flaw, evidence of an imperfect personality. If we are imperfect, why do we think we can achieve perfection?

Chasing the moving target of perfection will only make us crazy. Better to make peace with our imperfection and enjoy parenting for what it is—an imperfect, fascinating and rewarding job.

◊

I will discard the fantasy of perfection.

_____

_____

_____

_____

_____

July 29

CHILDHOOD

Childhood is a short season.

Helen Hayes

◊

Scan any crowd and you will find living proof that childhood is a short season. Grade school girls are wearing make–up and pre–teen boys dress like 18 year olds. Were these children ever children?

To short change children on childhood is to send them into the world with a handicap. Psychological maturity comes from experiencing and ages and stages of childhood. Nobody has found a substitute for childhood yet.

It is a mistake to allow youngsters to masquerade as adults. Using children as substitute adults is also a mistake. If we err, let us err on the side of childhood, a short, precious and necessary season.

◊

I will be aware of the shortness of childhood.

_____

_____

_____

_____

_____

July 30

CREATIVITY

The tender sprout of creativity needs to be encouraged and guided almost from birth.

Joan Beck

◊

Budding creativity is fragile and can easily be crushed—trampled to death. We need to be aware of our children's creativity and nurture it.

Creativity is a gift, an innate talent or talents bestowed upon our children. Their lives are richer and happier because of creativity. We water and fertilize the plants in our homes. Why not water and fertilize children's creativity?

Our children's creativity grows, buds and blooms into glorious color, like a field of wildflowers.

◊

I will nurture creativity in my children.

_____

_____

_____

_____

_____

July 31

FAMILY

In our family, in sickness and in health, we were all involved with one another, all in the same life, a continuum, a seamless fabric, a flow of time.

Rose Fitzgerald Kennedy

◊

Families serve as protective cocoons for children. A family does not have to be large in order to function. One parent and one child comprise a family.

The family name and generations of people who have shared that name form a continuum that transcends time. Our children experiment with different roles and behaviors within the family structure.

Giving our children a sense of family is one of the most thoughtful gifts we can ever give them.

◊

I will give my children a sense of family.

_____

_____

_____

_____

_____

August 1

SECURITY

The security of a parent about <u>being</u> a parent will eventually become the source of the child's feeling secure about himself.

Bruno Bettleheim, M.D.

◊

So many things about parenting make us feel anxious. We need to give ourselves credit where credit is due. Every day we are intuitive, adaptive, creative and loving parents.

In time parents are rewarded. As our experience grows, we feel more secure about parenting. While nothing in life is ever secure, we find security in the knowledge that we are doing the best we can. We feel more confident about being parents.

Our children sense this shift in our feelings and feel more secure about themselves. Security does not come easily to parents or children, but if we are patient, it comes.

◊

I will strive to feel secure about parenting.

_____

_____

_____

_____

_____

August 2

COMMUNICATION

If parents are any good at listening, they will begin to hear the heart.

James and Mary Kenney

◊

Many of us have perfected the skill of assumed listening. We look like we are listening, yet are quite unaware of what our children are saying. The message does not get from the sender to the receiver.

In order to close the communications loop, we need to pay close attention to our children's words and feelings. Feelings are the basis of communication. When we listen attentively to our children they feel comfortable about sharing their thoughts with us. Some of us are lucky enough to have children who share their dreams.

Good communication involves listening with our ears, our minds and most of all, our hearts. Heartfelt listening is heartfelt parenting.

◊

I will listen with my heart.

_____

_____

_____

_____

_____

August 3

FEELINGS

Children can't help feeling what they do.
                                        Nancy Samalin

◊

Have you ever gotten angry at yourself for getting angry? Or petty? Or embarrassed? Unfortunately, our emotions do not have on/off switches. We cannot always control our feelings, but we can learn to temper them.

Kids are the same way. They cannot help feeling the way they do. However, children can learn to identify their feelings and find ways of coping. We can help our children by treating their feelings as legitimate, being honest with our own feelings and showing unconditional love.

Together, parents and children can learn how to accept feelings and banish guilt. Feelings without guilt is a wonderful feeling!

◊

I will accept my children's feelings as legitimate.

_____

_____

_____

_____

_____

August 4

RELATIONSHIPS

The self–accepting person is able to give up on outgrown relationships without pain and to build new relationships without fear.

Dr. Mortimer Feinberg, Gloria Feinberg and John Tarrant

◊

Adaptation differs from acceptance. It is possible to adapt to the changing relationships we have with our children and never really accept them. We infantilize our children, clinging to dated relationships and resisting the formation of new ones.

Self–accepting parents know how to adapt to the changes in their children. Change is viewed as a positive force in children's lives. As one father commented, "My daughter was an interesting child. Today, as a married woman, she is a fascinating adult."

Changing family relationships make our lives richer, fuller and more beautiful.

◊

I will plan for the empty nest before it occurs.

_____

_____

_____

_____

_____

August 5

CONTROL

The other sobering thought for humans is how much joy goes on without us, how much life we have been unable, despite strong effort, to bring under our heel.

Bill Holm

◊

Some of us work so hard at controlling life, we miss the beauty that surrounds us.

My mother–in–law had a talent for finding joy and beauty everywhere. She thought the stark winter landscape had a special kind of beauty. "Isn't that barn a marvelous red?" she asked one day. The barn was so old it was leaning. The siding was riddled with holes and badly splintered. The red paint was barely visible, a few splotches on some of the boards. But there was an elusive quality about the paint, a hint of bygone days, of threshing bees and hearty farm suppers eaten beneath shade trees.

Were it not for Mom, I might have missed the faded red paint and the dignity of the old barn, standing proudly against the hills.

◊

I will forfeit control and enjoy my life.

August 6

PROBLEMS

If you have a big enough family, you'll get every problem there is.

Dr. Charles Mayo

◊

Our children have an amazing range of problems. Their problems become our problems. Some of the problems we deal with are beyond belief! Numbing.

Life—threatening problems require our immediate attention, whereas other problems can be worked on slowly. We chip away at them until they are gone. The solutions to some of our problems may appear to be mismatched. In retrospect, we see evidence of our Higher Power at work, prodding and helping us.

No matter how many problems we have, or the range of these problems, we need to balance them against the joys of life. Things usually work out. Solving problems is easier if we deal with them one at a time.

◊

I will work on one problem at a time.

_____

_____

_____

_____

_____

August 7

CHANGE

Life is constantly changing...my ideas are constantly changing.

Princess Grace of Monaco

◊

We are sure our ideas will withstand the test of time, until we discover time has changed our ideas. Our changing ideas and opinions are confusing to children.

The confusion clears when we tell our children we have changed our minds and give them a brief summary of our reasoning. Children need to develop a sense of cause and affect. Our disclosures help them to see cause—effect relationships and gives them tacit permission to change their minds.

Changing our ideas is a human response, proof we are adapting to the changes in our lives.

◊

I will admit when my ideas have changed.

_____

_____

_____

_____

_____

August 8

HOPE

What fantastic hope nourishes me?

Allen Wheelis

◊

All of us have times when we feel hopeless. We want to nourish hope and keep it alive, but how?

We can turn to our children. They divert our attention away from the problems at hand and help us to re–charge. It is hard to feel glum in the presence of our children. Even if our children are the root of our hopeless feelings, we can still find hope in remembering the happy times we shared with them.

Our children cannot, and should not, be the sole source of our hope. But they can help us to sustain hope. Children are the hope of the present and the future.

◊

I will find hope in my children.

_____

_____

_____

_____

_____

August 9

TOLERANCE

You are the only one who will benefit by striving to be tolerant.

Robert Conklin

◊

Tolerance is more than respect for the beliefs and actions of others, it is the process of determining variations. How much variation in our children's behavior can we accept?

Kids test our tolerance regularly. Our tolerance slips when we are confronted by disrespectful and irrational children. We need to give ourselves time to re–think things. If we are willing to make concessions, our children will probably be willing to make concessions. Parenting becomes more of a cooperative effort.

Every day our children work on maturity. We can be in–step with them by working on tolerance.

◊

I will be lovingly tolerant with my children.

_____

_____

_____

_____

_____

August 10

PERCEPTION

The art of good parenting begins with the fundamental skill of being able to get behind the eyes of a child.

Dr. James Dobson

◊

Years ago I saw a film which was taken from the perspective of a five year old child. Doorknobs looked like huge globes, adults looked like giants, everything was bigger than life.

The film demonstrated how intimidating an adult environment appears to young children. Afterwards, in speaking with kids, I always knelt down. The children knew what I was doing and smiled or hugged me. Communication between us was clearer because we were the same height.

Talking with our children is easier when we are eyeball to eyeball. Good parents try to view life through their children's eyes.

◊

I will try to see life through the eyes of children.

_____

_____

_____

_____

_____

August 11

RESPONSIBILITY

Effective parents give every child some household responsibility appropriate to his or her age.

Raymond Wlodkowski and Judith H. Jaynes

◊

Giving our children chores to do is an act of kindness. The kids feel needed and derive satisfaction from contributing to the family's welfare.

However, we need to match the right chores to the right children. Preschoolers can clean a sink. Highschoolers can help with cooking. In assigning chores to our children, we are really saying, "I trust you enough to ask you to help," a heady feeling for youngsters.

Knowing we are responsible people makes us feel good about ourselves. Kids are no different.

◊

I will help my children learn responsibility by assigning chores.

_____

_____

_____

_____

_____

August 12

LOVE

Love is union with somebody...under the condition of retaining the separateness and integrity of one's own self.

Erich Fromm

◊

Many of us make false assumptions about love. We think we have to give up ourselves in order to love others, or find ourselves torn between loving a mate and loving children. Neither of these responses justifies love.

To love someone is to accept them. By its very nature, love is a giving emotion. So why do we doubt love? The people who genuinely love us want us to retain our identities. Keeping a part of ourselves separate from others does not mean we love them less. It simply means we also love ourselves.

Children need to see us maintaining our identities so they can develop theirs.

◊

I will retain my identity while I love my children.

August 13

EMPATHY

We show caring when we are empathetic to our youngster's problems and weaknesses.

Linda Albert and Michael Popkin

◊

One of the best ways to show love for our children is to empathize with them. Nothing is quite as maddening to kids as a parent who glosses over problems with "there, there" behavior.

The preschooler who is terrified of dogs does not want to hear a lecture on the merits of man's best friend. He or she wants love, understanding, and protection. Feeling safe helps the child to come to grips with scary feelings.

Our children learn about empathy from us. If we empathize with their problems they will be more apt to empathize with ours. Empathy and love go hand in hand.

◊

I will be empathetic to my children's problems.

_____

_____

_____

_____

_____

August 14

TOY MAKING

When children make their own toys, or when parents help their children do so, it always produces the most gratifying results.

T. Berry Brazelton, M.D.

◊

There is something touching about simple toys, wooden blocks, large balls, teddy bears and paper kites. All of these toys demand action from our children.

Our children invent toys naturally. Their home-made toys are superior to manufactured toys because they are personal. More meaningful, too, because our children have taken the time to think through the design, construction and play aspects of toy–making. The soul of a child is in every toy.

No, our children don't need passive toys or whiz–bang electronics. They have more fun inventing their own toys. We can help them be children again, just for a little while.

◊

I will spark my children's creativity by making toys with them.

_____

_____

_____

_____

_____

August 15

FAMILY

We are always in the process of designing our descendents.
Willard Gaylin

◊

Life does not always go according to our plans. A kindergarten child may suffer from separation anxiety, or an adolescent may be abusing drugs. Both behaviors make parents feel anxious and worried.

Parenting has always been a process of designing one's descendents. Our goal is to turn out well–adjusted, responsible, productive and happy adults. This means we never give up on our children.

No matter how difficult or outrageous our children's behavior becomes, we need to be there for them. We do not always like our children, but we always love them. Our love, combined with the love of family members, is a lifeline to recovery.

◊

I will never give up on my children.

_____

_____

_____

_____

_____

August 16

STRESS

At times I wonder whether we haven't lost the power to screen the adult world for and from our children.

Ellen Goodman

◊

Daily news reports always include violent stories, the stuff of childhood stress. Vainly we try to screen these stories from our children.

The sheer volume of stories makes us feel powerless. But we are not powerless. We can monitor our children's television viewing, write letters to the editor, contact influential legislators and volunteer our services. Our collective voices can—and will—be heard.

As we strive to screen the adult world from our children, we also strive to be rational and calm. And we can make our homes into cozy, restful, happy and secure places for children.

◊

I will screen young children from violence.

_____

_____

_____

_____

_____

August 17

ADOLESCENCE

Slumber parties were not in my game plan for adult life.
                        Caryl Rivers and Alan Lupe

◊

Preparing for adolescent activities, slumber parties and the like, is easier than preparing for behaviors. The behavior of our adolescent children is challenging, to say the least. Will we survive?

Adolescence is a time of independence, intellectual leaps, shifting identities, and emerging sexuality, all in all, a lot for us to handle. We need to remember these behaviors are a lot for our children to handle, too.

Although our teenagers dress and behave like adults, they are actually trying out adulthood. At this busy time of life, we need to merge our plans with children's plans. Our teenagers really need us.

◊

I will merge my plans with adolescent plans.

_____

_____

_____

_____

_____

August 18

AWARENESS

I have learned to recognize the extraordinary things that even the most ordinary lives contain.

Rabbi Harold Kushner

◊

Ordinary things in nature make life beautiful. A cricket orchestra. Swirling fog. Geese flying in a "V" formation. Wild raspberries. Cumulus cloud shapes. Flashing fireflies. Rippling streams. Pink sunsets.

Ordinary things in parenting make life beautiful. Baby's first tooth. Rosy cheeks. Unsteady steps. A scribbled picture. Tidy bedrooms. Good school reports. Help with the dishes. Impulsive hugs.

Our awareness of beauty develops slowly. In time, we are able to discern the extraordinary things in our ordinary lives. Ordinary things are often miracles in disguise.

◊

I will look for the extraordinary things in my ordinary life.

_____

_____

_____

_____

_____

August 19

COPING

Parenting books have enduring popularity precisely because no one has yet come up with the answers.

Peggy Finston, M.D.

◊

The search for parenting answers is ongoing. Self–help and parenting books often contain lots of practical hints but have few substantive answers. That is because the authors do not know our children.

Each of us must find our own answers to parenting questions. Daily parenting forces us to confront our problems, be adaptive and craft solutions. The search for answers leads us to an important and crucial discovery: We can cope.

Nobody has come up with all the answers, nor would we want them to. We will find our own answers in our own time.

◊

I will identify my own ways of coping.

_____

_____

_____

_____

_____

August 20

FATHERS

When, after a cry, he stares at me with a critical and resentful gaze, I feel the mixed pride and oppression of fatherhood at the very base of my spine.

E.B. White

◊

The doubts we have about parenting can strike with hammer force. Can we do this? Can we do it well? Will our kids turn out okay?

Some worries are bona fide, based upon facts, whereas others are hunches, based upon feelings. A few anxious thoughts can turn into constant anxiety and feelings of oppression. We need to remember that our ancestors survived parenting and we will, too. The thought is comforting.

Whether we are fathers or mothers, parenting is easier if we take it one day at a time. Then too, we need to resist the desire to complicate things. We love our children and they love us. It's simple.

◊

I will handle fatherhood one day at a time.

_____

_____

_____

_____

_____

August 21

SELF–CONCEPT

I have no trouble convincing them that I'm their daddy, but sometimes I have trouble convincing them that I'm a comedian.

Bob Hope

◊

The need to justify ourselves to children is an intriguing quirk of human personality. We want our children to think our work is important and respect us for doing it.

Our needs may be ignored. Not all children are interested in their parents occupations. They are quite content to think of us as mere parents. And we must be content. Imposing our needs upon children adds tension to parent–child relationships.

We are the ones who validate ourselves. Our work. Our parenting. If we respect ourselves, our children probably will also.

◊

I will respect myself for what I do.

August 22

IMMEDIACY

For a period of time I lived fully in the present moment.
Catherine Marshall

◊

We think living in the present is automatic. Untrue. Living in the present is one of the toughest challenges parents face.

Some of us spend too much time in the past, with memories, wounds, guilt and, in some cases, grudges. Without realizing it, we have regressed. Like the dieter who relapses, we are tempted to indulge ourselves, go on a binge and wallow in our pain. All are self–defeating behaviors.

Living in the present requires honesty, courage and plain hard work. Children can help us. Their busy lives keep us tuned to the present. How fortunate we are to have this day to spend with our children.

◊

I will live in the present with my children.

August 23

SECURITY

Children are horribly insecure; the life of a parent is the life of a gambler.

Sydney Smith

◊

Every day of parenting is a gamble. So is life. None of us are born with assurances of happiness, good health or longevity. We may as well live life to the fullest. This means we take calculated risks.

Some risk–taking involves our children. We gamble that individual tutoring will help a child to become a competent reader. We gamble that drug treatment will help a young adult to become straight. We gamble that parenting will mold our children into productive citizens.

Gambling on our children is an endorsement, a vote of confidence, a way of showing faith in their abilities. Faith stacks the odds in our children's favor.

◊

I will take chances on my children.

_____

_____

_____

_____

_____

August 24

LOVE

With my heart poised in love, my emotional energy can never be drained by the challenging events in life.

Pearl Bailey

◊

Love is powerful. The love we feel we have for a mate and children, and their reciprocal love for us, acts like protective armor. We are protected from some of the painful events in life.

Love is brave. Because we love our children, we do things we are scared to do, take chances we would not ordinarily take, and work for causes we never dreamed of endorsing. We do these things because we want our children to have happy lives.

Love is giving. We care about our children more than we care about ourselves. Their sweet love inspires us. We accept the challenges of parenting with our hearts poised in love.

◊

I will keep my heart poised in love.

_____

_____

_____

_____

_____

August 25

CHILDHOOD

Very young children have an artless beauty, an innocent grace, an unstudied abandon of movement.

A.A. Milne

◊

Clever advertisers use children's pictures to get the public's attention. Why not? Children are natural, adorable, humorous, surprising and lively.

E.H. Shepard illustrated Milne's books. Shepard's simple pen and ink drawings helped to make the Pooh books famous. With just a few pen strokes, Shepard captured the artless beauty and unstudied movement of children. His drawings can help us to appreciate our children.

Our children are natural works of art, kinetic sculptures, beautiful in, and of, themselves. They are so beautiful it brings tears to our eyes.

◊

I will look at the unstudied grace of children with wonder.

_____

_____

_____

_____

_____

August 26

MINUTIAE

Perhaps it is the minutiae of life that makes us appreciate the rest of living.

Phyllis Naylor

◊

Ever noticed how the loud parts of a song are usually preceded by soft parts? The decrescendo makes the crescendo more exciting. So it is with the minutiae of life.

We would not appreciate the exciting passages of our lives without the minutiae. While our hands are busy, our minds are busy. Many of life's major problems are solved while we are peeling potatoes, folding laundry, and sweeping floors.

The minutiae of life is more important than we think. Instead of dreading mundane tasks, we should welcome them.

◊

I will take comfort in the minutiae of life.

_____

_____

_____

_____

_____

August 27

CHILD DEVELOPMENT

The trouble is that growing up is a full–time job.
                                        Peg Bracken

◊

Yes, parents can be self–centered. We can be so consumed by our problems that we don't see our children's problems.

Children are exposed to stress at an early age. The stress they feel is real and worrisome. When our children muster the courage to tell us about their stressful feelings, we minimize their feelings and tell "when I was your age" stories, just what they don't want to hear.

We think of parenting as a full–time job. Similarly, our children think of childhood as a full–time job. Parents and children can work together to get their jobs done. We can also try to understand each other.

◊

I will think of childhood as a full–time job.

_____

_____

_____

_____

_____

August 28

GUILT

I spent a lot of time today thinking how hard the last six years have been. I'm almost ashamed to admit that I feel I have deprived my family of so much.

Governor Mario Cuomo

◊

Guilt comes with parenting. We know we are going to make mistakes, but we do not really accept the fact. Why aren't we kinder to ourselves?

Bad things happen. If we could have foreseen the future we would have behaved differently. And if our children could have foreseen the future they would have behaved differently. The only thing we can do is accept our powerlessness.

Some parenting decisions are bound to make us feel guilty. However, we cannot allow guilt to consume us. Guilty, negative thoughts can be countered with secure, positive thoughts. We can do it!

◊

I will counter negative thoughts with positive ones.

_____

_____

_____

_____

_____

August 29

TALK

Children do not converse. They say things.
                                                    Charles Schulz

◊

One day I overheard a hilarious conversation. Two boys in my nursery school class, one tall and one short, were building a block tower. When the shorter boy added the last block to the tower it wobbled precariously and collapsed.

The tall boy threw his blocks down and stomped away. "You're a dinglepoop!" he shouted angrily.

The short boy stretched to his full height, put his hands on his hips, took a deep breath and countered, "Well, you're a banana."

Shock registered on the tall boy's face. On some invisible rating scale of childhood, being called a banana was worse than being called a dinglepoop. Every time I think of this conversation I smile.

◊

I will find humor in children's talk.

_____

_____

_____

_____

_____

August 30

COMMON SENSE

Mary and I had a very simple approach to raising our daughters, based on the common sense we had been taught by our own parents.

Lee Iacocca

◊

Common sense appears to be in short supply. We cannot stop ourselves from turning simple problems into complicated ones. Our common sense has deserted us.

One of the best things we can do for our children is to teach them about common sense. The ability to apply common sense will help them get through life. Some examples: If you don't put your toys away they may get broken. If you don't study for the math test you may fail. If you don't put gas in the car you could run out on a country road.

We teach our children by example when we apply common sense to parenting. Sounds sensible, doesn't it?

◊

I will apply common sense to parenting.

_____

_____

_____

_____

_____

August 31

FORGIVENESS

Forgiveness means letting go, moving on and favoring the positive.

Harold Bloomfield, M.D. and Leonard Felder, Ph.D.

◊

Forgiveness is a gradual process. It starts with identifying feelings, progresses to accepting feelings, letting go, moving forward with life and then concludes with a positive outlook. Unless we reach the last stage the process is incomplete.

Are you stuck on forgiveness? The failure to forgive our children is a personal failure. We wind up hurting ourselves. With each passing day, our children feel more estranged from us and we from them. Forgiveness is a small price to pay for sharing our lives with our children.

We can use forgiveness as a springboard to positive thinking. So can our children.

◊

I will use forgiveness as a springboard to positive thinking.

_____

_____

_____

_____

_____

September 1

EMPTY–NEST

The pain of the empty–nest syndrome is not diminished by the predictability of the event and the futility of resistance.
Mortimer Feinberg, Ph.D., Gloria Feinberg and John Tarrant

◊

Buying school supplies for my children made me sad. Both of my daughters would be attending school and I would be home alone.

My husband sensed my feelings and took me out to lunch on the first day of school. On the second day of school, however, things returned to normal. I prowled about the house nervously, wondering what to do next and feeling depressed by the silence. The predictability of the start of school did not lesson my pain.

With my husband's help, I was able to find new interests and adapt to my nearly empty nest.

◊

I will find new interests in life.

_____

_____

_____

_____

_____

September 2

LEARNING

No child who is learning is ever doubting that he is loved.
Polly Berrien Berends

◊

Learning is exciting for children. We get excited, too, watching our children grasp new skills and concepts.

We do not always understand the subjects our kids are studying. Still, we can encourage their learning. Unlike the father who shouted at his kindergarten child, "What are you trying to do, be smarter than your daddy?" This father could not come to terms with his child's learning or the things he was learning.

Encouraging our children's learning is a way of expressing our love. We want our kids to be educated and ready to face the future.

◊

I will encourage and support my children's learning.

_____

_____

_____

_____

_____

September 3

ROLE MODELS

The child says nothing but what it heard by the fire.
                                        Old Proverb

◊

Supper time talk can easily be misinterpreted by our children. When our garbled comments come back to us we are red–faced and embarrassed.

We continue to be role models for our children. Whether they are preschoolers or highschoolers, it is important for us to monitor our conversations. This is not censorship, but parental judgment. Exercising judgment is better than being misunderstood and/or misquoted.

Careful words are really caring words. Don't you think those are the best kind?

◊

I will be careful about what I say in front of children.

_____

_____

_____

_____

_____

September 4

COMMUNICATION

Speaking was impossible; no words could be heard in the uproar and nobody apparently cared to hear any.

Charles Lindbergh

◊

The noise level in the house is often so high, we cannot hear ourselves speak. The kids don't hear us either. What can we do?

Unless what we have to say is critical, we have the option of tabling family discussion. The tabling technique gives parents and kids time to think about what they want to say. Because we are unhurried and undistracted, family communication is better.

Speaking above the uproar is impossible. We can adapt to our children's needs and make appointments with them, if necessary, anything to encourage good communication.

◊

I will have quiet talks with my children.

_____

_____

_____

_____

_____

September 5

IMMEDIACY

Only by extracting, at each present time, the full meaning of each present experience are we prepared for doing the same thing in the future.

John Dewey

◊

We are happier—more alive—when we live in the present. The ability to live in the present is self–taught, a skill that comes with experience. Some of us never seem to get the hang of it.

Despite the lectures we give ourselves, we cannot find the courage to trust life. We wait for tragedy to strike. Why do we underestimate ourselves? From beginning to end, from moment to moment, this day is ours, to do with as we wish. Only when we discover the full meaning of today can we appreciate the meaning of tomorrow.

Every day contains something beautiful.

◊

I will enjoy this beautiful day.

_____

_____

_____

_____

_____

September 6

SUPPORT

We want to stay put as much as we can and support the kids' activities.

Goldie Hawn

◊

Parental support of children's activities takes many forms, from driving kids to a shopping mall to sitting on a stadium bench in freezing weather.

Support can be the difference between giving up and hanging in there. Our children need to know they can count on us, no matter what happens. We will support their failures. We will support their successes. In time, our children develop persistence—the courage to try again.

Our support gives children warm, fuzzy feelings. And we feel the same way.

◊

I will support my children's activities.

September 7

PETS

A pet is not only a child's best friend, it is also one of the most reliable allies parents have in raising their children to be emotionally stable and secure.

Maria Piers and Genieve Millet

◊

Kids and pets go together.

Taking care of pets helps children to understand the benefits of regular care. They learn about love, too, loving a pet and being loved in return, or at least appreciated. Hugging a pet makes our children feel good. That is one of the reasons pet therapy is being used in pediatric, psychiatric and geriatric care. You could say pet therapy begins at home.

Forget the mess. Forget the expense. Forget the trouble. Pets are our allies—part of the family.

◊

I will consider pets as parenting allies.

September 8

ALONENESS

Sometimes children want to be left in peace or to be alone with their feelings.

Nancy Samalin

◊

All children have times when they want to be alone. The reasons? They may be overtired, absorbed in make–believe, reading a good book, or sick of noise.

Those of us who fear aloneness may be upset by our children's desire for aloneness. We check up on our kids every few minutes and interrupt their solitude with small talk. Both actions show a lack of trust. If our children need time to be themselves, we need to be mature enough to give it to them.

Children have the right to privacy. Respecting our children's aloneness is another way of saying "I love you".

◊

I will respect my children's aloneness.

_____

_____

_____

_____

_____

September 9

CHANGE

All of our secret hopes come to the surface at the moment we decide to give up on the old and the known.

David Viscott, M.D.

◊

Change is easy to handle in small doses. Trouble comes when we handle too much, and change comes too fast.

The ability to handle change depends on our ability to relinquish control. We cannot control life and this realization is always scary. Life is forcing us to give up the known for the unknown. It is easier to handle change if we think of endings as new beginnings. One stage of life is phasing out, but it will be replaced by another.

We can handle change, along with our children and use it as an opportunity for growth.

◊

I will use change as an opportunity for personal growth.

_____

_____

_____

_____

_____

September 10

FAMILY

I was struck with the picture we made: Grandmothers, mothers, daughters, all of us playing out very traditional public roles.
Rosalynn Carter

◊

Usually grandparents, parents and children play traditional roles. We assume these are the only roles our family members know. We are wrong.

Life is filled with surprises, like the grandmother who suddenly decided to finish her college degree and graduated at the top of her class. These kinds of stories inspire us to play non–traditional roles: single parenting, crossing occupational barriers, sharing with childcare.

We can break with tradition and enjoy it. What a gift for our children!

◊

I will find the courage to break from traditional roles.

_____

_____

_____

_____

_____

September 11

AGING

The kind of things women go through about aging has to do with certain losses, not only because of what society does to women, but because of how women's bodies change.

Sally Field

◊

Men experience physical changes during middle–age, but nothing like the changes women undergo. Menopause and parenting are often at odds.

While estrogen therapy helps many menopausal women, women have also discovered they can help themselves. They know their creativeness is peaking and embrace life with a confidence and zest unknown to youth. Businesses are finding these qualities pay off.

Whether we are female or male, middle–aged or younger, we can maximize our talents, seize opportunities and make peace with aging. Life awaits.

◊

I will make peace with aging.

September 12

REALITY

Life, the reality you create, is nothing more and nothing less than you want it to be.

Barry Ellsworth

◊

Because their perceptions of reality are different, witnesses to the same crime often tell conflicting stories.

So it is with life. Our perceptions of reality differ and therefore our lives differ. Talent, personality and drive also affect our perceptions of reality. The reality of parenting is what we want it to be. We can choose to withdraw or risk. We can choose to complain or compliment. We can choose to be unhappy or happy.

Parenting is a series of choices. Nobody can make our choices for us.

◊

I will define my own reality.

September 13

HUMOR

When I requested my cocksure Lad to repeat our newly memorized Bible verse, "The Lord loveth a cheerful giver", Rolfe brought forth this astounding version: "God loveth a chick liver."
                                                    Alice Lee Humphreys

◊

Children's humor (intentional and accidental) helps us to keep life in balance. After a good laugh, our problems seem less important and some even fade away.

Word mistakes are an endless source of humor. We can't help but smile when we think about God loving chicken liver. Our laughter spreads like grains of wheat that have been winnowed on a windy day. The seeds of children's humor have been sown and pop up in the oddest places.

Our children's humor is delightful. Original. Quirky. Maybe God does like chicken liver. Who knows?

◊

I will keep my sense of humor handy.

_____

_____

_____

_____

_____

September 14

MATURATION

The kids are growing up and I don't like it.
Phyllis Naylor

◊

Some of us refuse to believe our children are growing up. We want them to be static, tiny figurines, ever young.

Do people get less interesting as they get older? No. They become more interesting and more interested in life. Our children are the same way. Each stage of childhood has its own characteristic charm. This becomes clearer to us as we observe the stages, enjoy our children, and continue to parent them.

Today is a good day to make a promise to ourselves. "I will accept my children's maturation." Say the promise three times to yourself. Maybe it will take.

◊

I will accept my children's maturation.

_____

_____

_____

_____

_____

September 15

POSSESSIONS

I wish I could show them (my children) how little they need to be happy.

Carol Burnett

◊

An old proverb says money cannot buy happiness. Our children do not believe the proverb. How could they? On week-ends we rush out to buy more stuff.

Happiness does not depend on possessions. Our children do not need more toys in order to feel happy. They do not need to be constantly entertained in order to feel happy. Certainly, they do not need to be spoiled in order to feel happy. They simply need to be loved.

We can help our children find alternatives to spending, such as creating, appreciating and giving. The happiest of times are the simplest of times.

◊

I will help my children learn to value people over possessions.

_____

_____

_____

_____

_____

September 16

HONESTY

The most important risk you can take is to be honest in expressing your feelings.

David Viscott, M.D.

◊

Some of us cannot express our feelings honestly. We think that expressing our feelings will make us look weak, insecure, even unstable.

Consider the alternatives. Stuffing feelings takes its toll on the human body over time. We may suffer from headaches, indigestion, ulcers, high blood pressure, miscellaneous aches and pains. Some of us have psychosomatic illness and mental depression. Our children do not understand us because they do not know us, which makes things worse. Everybody in the family suffers.

We are people, too, and have the right to express our feelings honestly.

◊

I will express my feelings honestly.

_____

_____

_____

_____

_____

September 17

PRIORITIES

I like going to bed at nine o'clock. I like watching TV, reading the paper and hanging around with my wife and just watching the baby.

John Goodman

◊

Parenting gives us new priorities and kids are at the top of the list.

Good intentions can be weakened by external forces, such things as work quotas, management policies, unexpected illness, financial problems and care of the the elderly. Keeping our priorities straight becomes harder and harder. Not keeping our priorities straight puts us at the mercy of random forces.

Sometimes parents have to take a stand. We can stay home tonight and play with our children.

◊

I will work at keeping my priorities straight.

_____

_____

_____

_____

_____

September 18

JOY

Most people do not give up on life because of a catastrophe. They give up because they no longer see the small joys worthy of celebration.

Robert Veniga

◊

Many of us miss the small joys of life when confronted by tragedy. We miss the small joys of parenting also.

A baby's first steps, shaky and insecure, are more than a small joy, they are a miracle of life. We are surrounded by similar miracles, if we would only open our eyes to them. Recovering from catastrophe begins with an awareness of the small joys of life and celebrating them.

Like kids on a treasure hunt, our children lead us to these joys. We can see how many joys we can find together. Being together is a joy.

◊

I will celebrate the small joys of parenting today.

_____

_____

_____

_____

_____

September 19

EXPERIENCE

I have always felt the more experiences a child has...the more interested in life he is likely to be.

Rose Fitzgerald Kennedy

◊

Some of us are stuck in a rut. Doing things with our children can rouse us from lethargy.

The newspaper contains many listings pertinent to children. Does your local library show children's films? How about riding the entire length of a bus route? Is there a cookie recipe in the paper you would like to try? Our children have all sorts of ideas.

Sharing experiences with our children makes life interesting. These experiences enrich our lives and are the stuff of memories.

◊

I will provide my children with varied experiences.

_____

_____

_____

_____

_____

September 20

PLAY

Winning or losing seems less important to children.
      Donald Medeiros, Barbara Porter and David Welch
◊

No rule of parenting says competitive parents have competitive children. Our children may be very different from us.

Deep in our hearts we know how our children feel. If our children are non–competitive, we can steer them away from the situations that are stressful for them. Many kids are happy simply observing, learning and participating. Participation itself has many rewards, not the least of which is friendship.

Non–competitive children need lots of playful times. We can make sure they get them.
◊

I will make sure my children have playful times.

_____

_____

_____

_____

_____

September 21

AMUSEMENT

It now costs more to amuse a child than it once did to educate his father.

Herbert Prochnow and Herbert Prochnow, Jr.

◊

We keep buying things for our children to keep them amused. The more we buy, the more they want.

Children can withstand boredom. Actually, a little boredom is good for them. Their imaginations take over. If you are a compulsive toy buyer, perhaps you need to examine the reasons for your behavior. Are you buying toys you always wanted but never had? Do you fear your children's boredom? Have you confused excessive giving with expressing love?

Boredom can be the mother of invention. Let your kids be inventive today.

◊

I will let my children amuse themselves.

_____

_____

_____

_____

_____

September 22

RESPONSIBILITY

My responsibility is to provide them a map, a lunch for the way and salve for bear scratches.

Ellen Walker

◊

With each passing year, we take our parenting responsibilities more seriously. There is such a thing, however, as being too responsible.

Our children need basics from us—food, clothing, shelter, love. They also need opportunities for growth. The father who builds his son's science project for him is doing him a disservice. His son would learn more about science by doing the project on his own. Assuming individual responsibility is a rite of passage for our children.

We can help our children and, at the same time, guard against being overly responsible. And we can keep the salve handy.

◊

I will take my parenting responsibilities seriously.

_____

_____

_____

_____

_____

September 23

FEELINGS

It's important to accept all our children's feelings, even the ugly ones.

Linda Albert and Michael Popkin

◊

We are never quite prepared for our children's verbal abuse.

The adolescent who screams at his mother, "I wish you were dead," is clearly out of control. Boiling feelings have erupted into hateful language. We need to be careful about overreacting to such behavior. An enraged adolescent needs time to calm down. A hurting parent needs time to think rationally. Adolescents feelings go up and down on a regular basis. Their roller–coaster emotions are part of growing up.

Sometimes our children have hateful feelings and we need to accept that. Children grow up and change.

◊

I will work on accepting my children's ugly feelings.

_____

_____

_____

_____

_____

September 24

PROBLEMS

For his own sake, and that of his child, a parent must solve problems as they occur and in his very own way.

Dr. Bruno Bettleheim

◊

Problems, problems, problems. All of us have problems. Should we ask for advice?

The Twelve Step Program encourages people to solve their problems by talking them out with others. Putting our problems into words is helpful, but we need to be aware of conflicting viewpoints, misinformation, tangential stories and projected emotions.

Comforting as group support may be, the solutions to our parenting problems must come from within us. Our parenting is tailored to our children.

◊

I will solve my own problems, in my own way.

September 25

DREAMS

Every mother has a secret dream for her child.
                                        Louise DeGrave

◊

Some of us think mothers have special dreams for daughters and fathers have special dreams for sons. This could be true.

We dream of school awards, successful careers, caring spouses, smiling grandchildren. Even if we do not speak about our dreams, we still have them. However, our children do not want our dreams foisted on them. They need to figure life out for themselves and dream their own dreams.

So we hold our dreams close to our hearts. Dreams are nothing more than loving thoughts about our children.

◊

I will continue to dream for my children.

_____

_____

_____

_____

_____

September 26

VALUES

Parents owe their children a set of decent standards and solid moral values around which to build a life.

Ann Landers

◊

Most of us know our values. The most determined parents, however, can waiver when pressured by children. Giving in to our kids is easier than arguing.

Moral values are like the North Star to children, a navigation point they will use throughout life. We need to make our values shine clearly. Words do not count as much as examples. Our children will figure out that we stand for honesty, hard work, caring and kindness. In later years they will remember these values.

We owe it to our children to identify—and live by—moral values. Life needs to be built on a firm foundation.

◊

I will live morally for myself and my children.

_____

_____

_____

_____

_____

September 27

SELF–WORTH

In the act of loving I am one with ALL and yet I am myself.
Erich Fromm

◊

Parenting takes a lot of stamina. Every day we react to our children's behavior. Every day we must regroup from all of the stresses of our day. This "react–regroup" pattern occurs so often it becomes routine.

As we take care of our children, we must take care of ourselves, or face burn–out. Taking care of ourselves is a pro–active response, a way of expressing self–love. We need not worry about running out of love.

Love replenishes itself. There is enough love inside each of us for everyone in the family, including ourselves. We love ourselves because we are worthy.

◊

I will love myself because I am worthy.

_____

_____

_____

_____

_____

September 28

CHILDCARE

My life is filled with cereal.

Phyllis McGinley

◊

Muddy footprints. Tangled hangers. Dirty clothes. Soggy cereal. Childcare messes can drive us nuts. While we are cleaning up one mess the kids are making another.

The end result of all these messes is camouflage. We cannot see past the messes to the beauty of parenting. Unless we adjust our vision, messes will be all that we see. Our children do not deserve this and neither do we. Although our lives look as if they are filled with cereal, they are really filled with love.

Work will always be waiting but our children will not. Just for a while, let us slam the door on messes and go out with our kids. It is time to look beyond the images of soggy cereal to the beauty of parenting.

◊

I will look beyond the images of soggy cereal to the beauty of parenting.

_____

_____

_____

_____

_____

September 29

POSITIVES

A *soft answer turneth away wrath: but grievous words stir up anger.*

Holy Bible, Proverbs 15:1

◊

This Bible verse could be applied to conversation. How often do we choose negative words to speak with our children?

Children's lives are filled with don'ts. Don't pester your sister. Don't pick the flowers. Don't get your clothes dirty. Don't touch that vase. Don't get the dog excited. The continuous barrage of negative words makes kids feel unworthy. What would happen if we changed the don'ts to do's?

Positive words can have positive results. Our children learn how to play with a sibling, pick selected flowers, have fun in the sandbox and respect beautiful things. See how many do's you can use today.

◊

I will use positive words whenever I can.

_____

_____

_____

_____

_____

September 30

CONSEQUENCES

Would we live differently, would we behave differently and choose differently if we understood that the consequences of what we choose to do will exist forever?

Rabbi Harold Kushner

◊

Some of us worry so much about the consequences of our parenting that we are totally ineffective.

Worry governs our days. We worry about what we did, what we did not do, what we saw, what we did not see, what we said, what we did not say and more. Compulsive worrying does not help our children. It is better to make sensible decisions, live with them and move on with life.

We do not have to be super heroes in order to be good parents.

◊

I will behave like a parent to my child.

_____

_____

_____

_____

_____

October 1

SUPPORT

Parents must continue to give their child physical immunization, but they can also give them emotional immunization as well.

Dorothy K. Whyte

◊

Careful as we are about our children's physical immunity, we are often casual about their emotional immunity. We think the kids will pick up the immunity just by hanging around the house.

Our children need emotional immunity as much as they need physical immunity. Emotional immunity, or support, differs from overprotective parenting. All of us need help at different times in our lives. Children especially need help in times of change. We can help our kids get over the rough spots and get back on track.

The emotional immunity we provide may be as simple as listening. Talking things out helps our kids to work things out.

◊

I will give my children emotional support when they need it.

_____

_____

_____

_____

_____

October 2

GROWTH

Grow up together, constantly.

Leo Buscaglia, Ph.D.

◊

Parents can act like children. In fact, we would probably be happier if we reverted to childhood more often.

Swinging with our children on an autumn afternoon is a good example. Flying over the tree tops, pumping our legs in tandem, is plain, old–fashioned fun. The soothing back and forth rhythm makes our problems seem less crucial. Our kids are delighted to see us acting like children, growing up with them.

Our children also learn a secret about us—parents really are kids at heart.

◊

I will bond with my children by growing up with them.

_____

_____

_____

_____

_____

October 3

UNIQUENESS

I've grown to understand that I must compare myself only to my own uniqueness, that I am a whole person, not different from others, because everyone, in a sense, has a part missing.
Rabbi Krauss and Morrie Goldfischer

◊

How easy it is to dwell upon weakness. If we are to be good parents, we must accept our weaknesses and make the most of our strengths.

Everybody lacks something. These missing parts make us unique and join us with the human family. Accepting our uniqueness helps our children learn to accept theirs. In coming to terms with our uniqueness we often develop new strengths. We learn to appreciate the talents we have been given.

Why waste time comparing ourselves to others? Our uniqueness makes us who we are, parents and children who love each other.

◊

I will find strength in my uniqueness.

_____

_____

_____

_____

_____

October 4

CRITICISM

Parents may be criticized for anything, with one exception—their children's behavior.

Brendan Francis

◊

The smallest criticism of our children's behavior ignites our anger. We interpret criticism of our children as criticism of our parenting. Anger clouds our judgment.

Many children behave differently away from home. Often parents are the last to know their kids are in trouble, especially the parents of drug–using kids. We need to check–out the stories we hear. Are the stories based on truth?

Over–reacting to criticism wastes valuable time. Our defensive behaviors divert us from the real problems and enable sick kids to get even sicker. Better to respond maturely to criticism and use our abilities to help our children.

◊

I will respond to criticism of my children maturely.

_____

_____

_____

_____

_____

October 5

TOUGHNESS

Being tough means you care.

Alan Loy McGinnis

◊

Because we care about our children, we set certain standards for their behavior. Growing children, particularly adolescents, test these standards regularly.

We must "hang tough." Children are confused by indecisive and/or lax parenting. Adolescents are looking for structure from us. They want us to prove our love by enforcing rules and risking their displeasure. In addition to enforcing house rules, we can help our children find alternative ways of coping.

Parenting is a tough job. We are tough enough— and we love our kids enough—to do it.

◊

I will demonstrate love for my children by being a tough parent.

_____

_____

_____

_____

_____

October 6

KINDNESS

A parent doesn't have to be a paragon of all the virtues—only a decent, kind person who is reasonably approachable.

Benjamin Spock, M.D.

◊

Kindness is often undervalued. When a person lacks kindness, however, we notice it immediately.

Our children need to know we are kind people. We are kind to them, their grandparents, their friends, their pets. Trust is the corollary to kindness in our children's eyes. They see our acts of kindness and conclude we are trustworthy parents.

Good parents need not be paragons of all virtues. We can be decent, kind, approachable people. A little kindness goes a long way.

◊

I will try to be approachable to my children.

_____

_____

_____

_____

_____

October 7

TIME

We feel it's more important to spend the whole day with our kids than spending a few hours with them.

Kurt Russell

◊

Nature or nurture? The debate between genetics and child rearing has persisted for years.

Rather than arguing about the issue, we can focus upon one truth: Children feel special when we spend time with them.   We need to give our kids as much un–interrupted time as possible.   Children do not perceive events as we do and may think of time and love as equals.

Spending a day with our children is a win–win situation. Everyone in the family feels loved.

◊

I will spend as much time with my children as I can.

_____

_____

_____

_____

_____

October 8

CONTROL

I'm beginning to trust life and go on without my having to control it.

Phyllis Chesler

◊

Life cannot be controlled like clay, formed and fired into shape. We try to control life anyway.

If we must control something, perhaps we should work at controlling ourselves. All of us have personality traits we could improve upon, things like nagging, procrastination, self–pity and addictive behaviors. The changes we make can have far–reaching affects. We trust life more because we trust ourselves more.

Trying to control life is a waste of effort.

◊

I will work at controlling myself and not life.

_____

_____

_____

_____

_____

October 9

NICKNAMES

Stop calling any child of ours "Billy." When you referred to "Billy" in previous letters I thought you meant some rather unfortunately named dog or cat.

Joyce Kilmer

◊

Nicknames are funny. Call a child a nickname once and it sticks. However, our kids may not be thrilled by their nicknames.

Childhood nicknames do not always translate to adulthood. Our children will tell us if they dislike their nicknames. We need to respect their feelings and address our children by the names they prefer. Nicknames may be loving names but they do not always sound that way.

Caring parents respect their children and their children's names.

◊

I will choose my children's nicknames carefully.

_____

_____

_____

_____

_____

October 10

FAILURE

Failure can only render us powerless if we let it.
                    Carole Hyatt and Linda Gottleib
                    ◊

We can be our worst enemies. Attitudes can cause us to snatch defeat from the jaws of victory.

Until we risk, we never know what we can do. Isn't it better to risk failure than never to risk at all? Failure renders us powerless only when we surrender to it. There are many things we can learn from failure, not the least of which is coping.

If we give ourselves enough time, we can grow from failure. This is one case when time is on our side.

                    ◊

I will give myself time to grow from failure.

_____

_____

_____

_____

_____

October 11

MOTHERS

A mother is the only thing that is so constituted that they possess eternal love under any and all circumstances.

Will Rogers

◊

Mothers are fountains of love. The more our children misbehave the more we love them.

Our love is tenacious, limitless and unconditional. A good thing, too, because sometimes love is the only option parents have left. Love ties us to our children. No matter what our kids have done, or how much trouble they are in, love is the connection that brings them back.

Love endures beyond time.

◊

I will give my children enduring love.

_____

_____

_____

_____

_____

October 12

GRIEF

The grief of a child is always terrible.

                                        Maria von Trapp

◊

Kid's emotions are close to the surface. Our children can be laughing one minute and grieving the next.

They mourn the death of pets, broken toys, shaky friendships, all sorts of things. Witnessing our children's grief is a terrible experience. We wish we could spare our children grief. But parents cannot experience grief for their children, nor should we. Grieving helps our children to appreciate life.

All we can do is console our children and love them. That is enough.

◊

I will console my children in times of grief.

_____

_____

_____

_____

_____

October 13

DIRECTION

You need moments, spaces in time, to be by yourself, to connect with your feelings and find your inner sense of direction.
Barry A. Ellsworth

◊

Only in quiet do we hear our thoughts.

We organize our thoughts more logically, thinking in complete sentences, putting periods on our sentences and grouping the sentences into paragraphs. Collecting our thoughts helps us get in touch with our feelings. The course of our parenting becomes clearer.

We need time away from our children just to think. Our thoughts lead us in the most amazing directions.

◊

I will use quiet times to redirect myself.

_____

_____

_____

_____

_____

October 14

STRUGGLE

Give your children the privilege of struggling.
                                    Mary Susan Miller
                              ◊

The road to achievement is paved with struggle. Our children must learn this if they are going to live rewarding lives.

Kids appreciate things more if they have worked to attain them. Our children learn about planning and budgeting and hard work. Striving to earn a bike makes its purchase even sweeter. The small struggles of childhood prepare our kids for the big struggles of life.

So let your children work toward something. A little struggle is good for the soul.
                              ◊

I will allow my children to struggle.

_____

_____

_____

_____

_____

October 15

LETTING GO

Happiness is easy. It is letting go of unhappiness that is hard.
Hugh Prather

◊

Happiness may be defined as a cooperation with pain. Seemingly happy parents still have pain in their lives.

Some of us have children who are truants, delinquents, alcoholics, drug addicts, runaways, criminals and more. These problems are a blight on our lives. Pain prods our psyches, makes us more aware, and forces us to cherish life. How do we find happiness?

We make the conscious decision to let go of unhappiness. Life is too precious to waste.

◊

I will continue to work at letting go.

_____

_____

_____

_____

_____

October 16

ADOLESCENCE

How a teenager behaves depends very much on how he behaved before he was a teenager.

Princess Grace of Monaco

◊

Adolescents differ. Some have trouble getting through the teenage years, while others breeze right through them.

The parents of polite, hardworking, goal–oriented teenagers often say this behavior started in infancy. These parents never had much trouble with their kids. Parenting adolescents is easier if we tailor our techniques to our kids.

Most of all, we need to keep our cool with teenagers. All of us have our crazy days.

◊

I will keep my cool when parenting adolescents.

_____

_____

_____

_____

_____

October 17

MIRACLES

Miracles happen only to those who believe in them.
                                    French Proverb

◊

My mother always wanted an apple tree. Dad finally bought her a small sapling and, for some unknown reason, planted it smack–dab in the center of the back yard.

The tree looked like a rake handle in the dirt. Certainly, it would be years before the tree bore fruit. Mom waited and waited. One night Mom had waited long enough. Under the cover of darkness, she tied shiny red apples onto the tree. In the morning she called the neighbors to tell them of the "miracle."

The neighbors laughed heartily when they saw the tree. Every time Dad, my brother and I looked out the kitchen window we laughed. Joke or not, a real miracle had occurred, the miracle of laughter.

◊

I will look for the miracles in my life.

_____

_____

_____

_____

_____

October 18

PERCEPTION

To live your life in the hope of getting unqualified approval from your child is to give far too much power to the child.
                              Dr. Jim Mastrich and Bill Birnes
◊

Kids seek approval. Parents seek approval, too, and some of us are neurotic about it. In subtle and blatant ways we look for approval from our children.

Our enabling behaviors, everything from letting kids run the show to buying them off, grants excessive power to minors. We are the parents in charge of our children. Sure, our happiness is affected by our children's feelings, but it does not depend upon them.

We strive to imbue our children with confidence. What about our confidence as parents? Confidence begins with self–approval.

◊

I will seek my own approval.

_____

_____

_____

_____

_____

October 19

EQUALITY

Parents and kids are not equal.
        Phyllis & David York and Ted Wachtel
                ◊

Although our children have legal rights, they do not have equal rights.

Time will never alter the fact that we are the parents and they are the children. Because we are older than our children, more educated than our children, we have more life experience to draw upon. Our parenting decisions are based upon experience. One decision, for everyone: While our children live with us they will abide by our rules.

Our children need to know the difference between rights and equal rights. We are the ones in charge.

                ◊

I will differentiate between rights and equal rights.

_____

_____

_____

_____

_____

October 20

HOUSEKEEPING

If a task is once begun.
Never leave it till it's done.
Be the labor great or small,
Do it well or not at all.

Anonymous

◊

     Housekeeping never ends. We start one job, are interrupted by our kids and get diverted to another job.

     However, we can try to complete a job once we have started it. Doing a job well the first time can save us follow–up time later. Our children can help us with the housekeeping chores. We all feel better living in a neat, clean place.

     While we work together, we enjoy each other's company. Busy hands really do make light work.

◊

I will try to do the little jobs of housekeeping well.

_____

_____

_____

_____

_____

October 21

LIMITS

We can't be all things to all people or try to do everything that comes along.
Harold Bloomfield, M.D. and Leonard Felder, Ph.D.

◊

Parents can feel down, disheartened and burdened by responsibility. Trying to be model parents wears us out.

This is the time to set limits. Setting limits helps us to figure out what is important in our lives. Our options include sharing responsibility, inactive status, cutting back on volunteerism, helping at a later date and, if necessary, resigning from groups.

Whether we are new or experienced parents, we have to take care of ourselves. Our survival depends on it.

◊

I will set reasonable limits for myself.

_____

_____

_____

_____

_____

October 22

ACCEPTANCE

Why do we struggle so hard to understand what has happened to us?

Jim Klobuchar

◊

Some of us analyze the past to the exclusion of everything else. We play mind games and find explanations for everything, a process family counselors call intellectualizing.

Not only is intellectualizing a waste of time, it is regressive behavior. Ultimately family relationships suffer. *The Serenity Prayer* asks for help in accepting things we cannot change. Our family history cannot be changed. We can.

◊

I will accept the past and move on with life.

_____

_____

_____

_____

_____

October 23

DISCIPLINE

One may reject the child's actions without rejecting the child.
       Dr. Rudolf Dreikurs and Pearl Cassel
                              ◊

Discipline may be the hardest lesson of child-hood. How to discipline may be the hardest lesson of parenting.

We must find ways of rejecting our children's behavior without rejecting our children. Words help us here, clear, short words our children can readily understand. "I'm angry about the smashed car, but thankful you were not hurt," for example.

Of course, discipline works best when combined with love. The roughest, toughest, most outrageous kids like to be hugged.

                              ◊

I will temper discipline with thoughtful words and hugs.

_____

_____

_____

_____

_____

October 24

QUIET TIME

The parents know their child needs solitude and quiet.
                                              Joseph Chilton Pearce

◊

Anyone who has visited a hospital nursery knows individual differences are present at birth. Some babies look cranky and hyper, others look quiet and serene.

Parents know which kids are which. Because gentle children tend to remain in the background, it is easy for us to overlook them. We must be careful not to go against the nature of these children and make sure they have enough quiet time.

Gentle children are special and should be treated as such.

◊

I will ensure that my quiet, gentle children have quiet, gentle times.

_____

_____

_____

_____

_____

October 25

SELF–ESTEEM

No child has too much self–esteem.

Nancy Samalin

◊

Every childhood experience teaches a child something about himself/herself. Our children identify their strengths, admit their weaknesses and speculate on potential. The ability to gauge competency is ongoing; it develops in childhood and continues throughout life.

Sometimes our kids get swelled heads but their conceit is short–lived. The cocky teenage driver learns to drive defensively after a few fender–benders. We foster our children's self–esteem by being honest with our feelings, showing confidence in their abilities and giving them our love.

◊

I will foster self–esteem in my children.

_____

_____

_____

_____

_____

October 26

CREATIVITY

A parent who talks happily with a small child—and listens seriously in return—is helping creativity to grow.

Joan Beck

◊

Children's thoughts leapfrog about so quickly we cannot keep pace with them. We still need to listen to our kids.

Listening tells our children we take them, and their ideas, seriously. Our children's conversation are very direct. We get a glimpse of their magical world as they try out humor, admit their fears and describe their dreams.

We may not be able to keep up with our children's creativity, but we can encourage it by listening to them.

◊

I will encourage my children's creativity by listening.

_____

_____

_____

_____

_____

October 27

WORRY

Worry: *be gone.*

Catherine Marshall

◊

While we cannot eliminate worry from our lives, we can take steps to keep it from getting out of hand.

First, we can guard against maximizing our worries. Once we become alert to maximizing we can spot it quickly. Second, we can sort facts from feelings. (The two are quite different.) Third, we can concentrate on the positives in our lives.

None of these steps is a cure–all. But they can make us feel a whole lot better.

◊

I will take conscious steps to control my worries.

_____

_____

_____

_____

_____

October 28

CONNECTEDNESS

Let a man once begin to think about the mystery of his life and the links which connect him with the life that fills the world, and he cannot but bring to bear upon his own life...the principle of Reverence for Life.

Albert Schweitzer

◊

Albert Schweitzer was so respectful of life he would not kill anything, not even a bee. Parents who have had a critically ill child understand his philosophy.

Our child's brush with death reminds us of the fragility of life. The life of a child is more important than their behavior. Overcome as we are by feelings of love, we have to keep working at letting go. In time, our children will take charge of their lives, respect our lives and understand that life is a precious gift.

"Reverence for Life" is a philosophy for parents and children alike, the tie that binds us together.

◊

I will connect with my children by showing a "Reverence for Life".

_____

_____

_____

_____

_____

October 29

PRAISE

If I could start parenthood over again—and I wish I could—the biggest change I would make is in stroking. Out loud.
Phil Donahue

◊

As important as praise is, the timing of praise is equally important. Praise has far less meaning after the fact.

Our children need constant approval from us. Excessive praise, however, sounds saccharin and may be ignored by our children. Honest and succinct are two words to remember when praising children. We can praise our children for so many things.

Today is the perfect day to give our children some heartfelt—and heartwarming—praise.

◊

I will praise my children today.

_____

_____

_____

_____

_____

October 30

AWARENESS

One of the things I like most about having her around is that she makes me notice things I had always taken for granted.
Bob Greene

◊

The wonder of babies is the wonder of discovery. Babies discover that Jell-O jiggles, milk splatters, doggies lick, flowers crush, beads tangle, whiskers scratch and birds chirp. All of these things have probably been forgotten by parents.

The wonder of parenting is the wonder of discovery. We rediscover the world with our children. They lead us to new friendships and experiences. We share our newfound awareness of life with other parents. Nothing about babies is taken for granted, except, perhaps, dirty diapers.

◊

I will notice the world of children and not take things for granted.

_____

_____

_____

_____

_____

October 31

BEAUTY

People who judge other people on externals don't realize that inner beauty is more important than anything else.

Cher

◊

It takes time to develop an appreciation of beauty.

We need to emphasize inner beauty to our children whenever possible. A physically disadvantaged child still has a sense of humor, fair play, kindness, intellectual curiosity and personal goals. These qualities, which some call character, contribute to the child's inner beauty.

Outer beauty fades in time. Inner beauty is everlasting.

◊

I will teach my children about inner beauty.

_____

_____

_____

_____

_____

November 1

STORIES

Parenthood is an endless list of truisms and folk tales that nobody ever gets tired of repeating.

Tom Bodett

◊

Our children's experiences are grist for story telling. Story topics include teething, toilet training, walking, playing, and learning. These parenting tales—and some are tall tales, to be sure—make us feel close to other parents.

Others may tire of hearing our parenting stories, but we never tire of telling them. The stories we recount are part of our family's oral history. Telling stories makes us relive our parenting experiences and we feel happy all over again.

◊

I will enrich our family's history with story telling.

_____

_____

_____

_____

_____

November 2

DEMANDS

The demands we make on ourselves are often deeply internalized "musts" others have imposed on us—usually early in childhood.

Sonya Friedman, Ph.D.

◊

Wow, we make trouble for ourselves. Our self-imposed demands can be far worse than the demands of others. Are we responding to current events or to stresses from our childhood?

Until this question is answered, we need to be cautious about making self-imposed demands. We can attain our parenting goals only if we are kind to ourselves. Above all, we want to have time to enjoy our children.

◊

I will make reasonable demands of myself.

_____

_____

_____

_____

_____

November 3

SEASONS

The poetry of earth is never dead.

John Keats

◊

Some of us dread winter. Yet, each season has a character and poetry that sets it apart. Crisp mornings, golden tamarack trees, icy streams, migrating birds and azure evening skies are sonnets in themselves.

The poetry of earth is ever-changing. If we work hard, we can train ourselves to see the subtlest changes in nature. Our imaginations add verses to the poetry of winter. We are comforted by the fact that winter is right on schedule. So get out the boots and smile!

◊

I will look for the poetry in the winter landscape and find comfort in it.

_____

_____

_____

_____

_____

November 4

GUIDANCE

I am being driven forward in an unknown land.
                                        Dag Hammarskjold

◊

Sometimes parenting feels like a journey to an unknown land. We are a million miles from home and in need of an experienced guide. Who will help?

Many guides are available, grandparents, other parents, friends, physicians, teachers, clergy, to name a few, and each guide has special insights. The exciting thing about the parenting journey is that our children accompany us. Our destination is a magical place called family.

◊

I will ask for guidance on my parenting journey.

November 5

HOPE

There are no hopeless situations in life; there are only people who have lost hope.

Rabbi Pesach Krauss and Morrie Goldfischer

◊

How can we recover from crisis? We can start by admitting we are powerless over life.

Powerlessness is a humbling feeling. Humility forces us to rethink our goals and find reasonable ways of achieving them. A sense of peace comes over us. There are no hopeless situations in parenting, only hopeless parents. The solutions we come up with are surprising.

We feel better when we bypass self-pity and concentrate on hope.

◊

I will seek hopeful solutions.

_____

_____

_____

_____

_____

November 6

MOTHERS

What greater aspiration and challenge are there for a mother than the hope of raising a great son or daughter?
                                        Rose Fitzgerald Kennedy

◊

Mothers have aspirations for their children. Some of our maternal aspirations clash with reality. A teenager drops out of school and our dreams shatter like glass.

We must not allow aspiration to escalate into frantic ambition. Our children have independent goals and timetables for these goals. The high school drop-out may come to value an education and graduate at a later date. Although our aspirations differ from our children's aspirations, it is exciting to watch them pursue their goals.

◊

I will encourage my children to pursue their goals.

_____

_____

_____

_____

_____

November 7

FAILURE

Share with your children the pain of failure.
                                    Mary Susan Miller
◊

Every rule has its exceptions. Failure is the exception to the rule about yammering to kids.

I spent nearly a year writing a 50,000 word book. The finished manuscript was not salvageable—a whopping failure. Because my daughters helped me plan the book, I called and told them why I had failed and how I was feeling. Immediately I started another writing project.

My daughters learned new things about me as they watched me rebound from failure. "I can't believe how well you are taking this," one said. The pain of failure brought me close to my children.
◊

I will talk with my children about failure.

_____

_____

_____

_____

_____

November 8

HONESTY

We will be as honest as we can with our children about everything!

Charlie Shedd

◊

Kids have their own communication network. The messages children send through this network, particularly young children, are often inaccurate. What plots!

Being honest with our children is crucial. We can set aside time to explain things, giving our children the basics without burdening them with a flurry of details. Facing life honestly takes courage. Parents and kids can start by being honest with each other.

◊

I will try to be honest with my children.

_____

_____

_____

_____

_____

November 9

BALANCE

Life has a way of balancing itself.

Valerie Harper

◊

We have all wanted something badly and been disappointed when we did not get it. Later we decide things worked out for the best.

The retrospective view of life is usually the clear view. Despite the chaos, the rushing, the minutiae, the unfairness, the pain, life has a way of balancing itself. Watching us cope helps our children to develop ways of coping.

In time, our children will become aware of the balance and order in their lives.

◊

I will be aware of the balance and order of life.

_____

_____

_____

_____

_____

November 10

NATURALNESS

What interests me is what children do at a particular moment in their lives when there are no rules, no laws, when emotionally they don't know what is expected of them.

Maurice Sendak

◊

Young children act impulsively and naturally—they do the unexpected. By the end of elementary school, however, much of our children's naturalness has diminished.

Our children have learned about manipulation and prejudice and peer pressure. Against these tough odds, we must encourage natural behavior in our children. Natural behavior is another way of saying, "I have the confidence to be myself."

◊

I will encourage my children to act naturally.

_____

_____

_____

_____

_____

November 11

WEAKNESS

I wanted you (children) to see me strong, so I hid my weakness.

Roseanne Barr

◊

It is as difficult for us to reveal weakness to our children as it is for them to reveal weakness to us.

Why do we try to be invincible? Parents must be strong for their children, we rationalize. Yes, strength comforts our children, but so does weakness. We are not fictional super-heroes, but vulnerable and weak, like everyone else.

Exposing our weakness to children ties the knot of love even tighter.

◊

I will expose my weakness for my children.

_____

_____

_____

_____

_____

November 12

MENTAL HEALTH

Life will always have its share of difficulties, in the midst of which you can choose to be satisfied, loving, and healthy.
Harold Bloomfield, M.D. and Leonard Felder, M.D.

◊

Many of us are handling major crises as we parent. How can we do both?

We can monitor our behavior and consciously decide to lead a satisfying life. This decision affects our perception of life. Unhealthy behaviors are gradually replaced by healthy behaviors, depressing thoughts are replaced by optimistic ones.

Being alert to happiness makes us happier. Our children feel happier, also.

◊

I will choose healthy decisions over unhealthy ones.

_____

_____

_____

_____

_____

November 13

QUIET TIME

Dearest son: it would be more pleasure if we could be together just in quiet, in some plain way of living . . .
                                                    Walt Whitman

◊

In the quiet times of life we get to know our children. Words are unnecessary. We understand each other intuitively.

And we understand, our children will grow up and leave us. Aloneness need not be our undoing. We can draw upon happy memories and find new ways of interacting with our children. Perhaps we choose even plainer ways of living.

Quiet times are critical to parenting. They help us figure out where we have been and where we are going.

◊

I will include quiet times in my life.

_____

_____

_____

_____

_____

November 14

ADOLESCENTS

To have children in their teens is to know you are living.
Sam Levenson

◊

Complex. Energetic. Unpredictable. Funny. Idealistic. These words and more have been used to describe adolescents.

We do not always understand our adolescents, but we can draw energy from them. To parent teenagers is to know we are alive. If nothing else, teenagers keep us from being complacent. Not resting on our laurels.

Every day of parenting quivers with excitement. Surviving our children's adolescence may be the ultimate challenge. Ready, get set, go!

◊

I will draw energy from my adolescents.

_____

_____

_____

_____

_____

November 15

TRENDS

At the moment, child—rearing is swinging in the direc-tion of self-conscious overemphasis.

Helen Hayes

◊

Parenting is awash in trends. Some of us have interpreted the permissiveness trend as submissiveness. We stuff our feelings and placate our children—anything to keep peace.

Submissive behavior is harmful to our children, who become more selfish and demand instant gratifica-tion. Life does not work this way. Many things, such as the development of a child's musical talent, cannot be rushed.

Parenting is not a popularity contest. We can cull the best from trends and follow our instincts.

◊

I will learn from trends and follow my parenting instinct.

_____

_____

_____

_____

_____

November 16

LOVE

To grow, to be reborn, one must remain vulnerable, open to love.
                                                    Anne Morrow Lindberg

◊

Our children hurt us. Some parents have actually been abused by their children.

One mother's teenage son tried to kill her. High on drugs, the son held his mother at gunpoint, spewed insults at her, changed his mind, and put the gun down. This was a traumatic experience for both mother and son. Because the mother remained open to love, she was able to get professional help for her son and forgive him.

In a sense, both mother and son were reborn. Love prevailed over violence.

◊

I will remain open to love.

_____

_____

_____

_____

_____

November 17

ADULT CHILDREN OF ALCOHOLICS

It's so tempting to clean up all the relatives my children see and hear about.

Ellen Walker

◊

Parents who are Adult Children of Alcoholics—and there are millions of us—may be inclined to keep the secret. Or down–play it. We do not want to dredge up old pain.

However, our children need to know their grandparents are active or recovering alcoholics. Our parent's alcoholism influenced who we are and could influence who our children will become. Tempted as we are to clean up our relatives, we must resist temptation and let the truth speak for itself.

We cannot change our relatives or get sober for them.

◊

I will tell my children that alcoholism is in their family tree.

_____

_____

_____

_____

_____

November 18

DISCIPLINE

The worst thing you can do in reprimanding children is to indicate the nature and degree of your desperation.

Jean Kerr

◊

Children lure us into dumb arguments. Nothing pushes our anger buttons faster than toddler behavior, the kind that degenerates into a test of wills.

Joining in on this behavior is an act of desperation. Youngsters sense our desperation and may be frightened by it. We can refuse to participate in dumb arguments. Instead of screaming, we can speak softly. Instead of bickering, we can give our kids time to calm down.

We discipline our children because we love them. "No" is a loving, caring word.

◊

I will discipline my children without resorting to desperate tactics.

_____

_____

_____

_____

_____

November 19

ANGER

It *requires courage to know when we are angry and let others hear it.*

Harriet Goldhor Lerner, Ph.D.

◊

Some of us are comfortable with our anger, while others have not come to terms with it.

It takes courage, not to mention an honest psyche, to accept the anger within us. Telling our children when and why we are angry helps them to understand anger. Our children are stronger than we think. We survived our parent's anger and they will, also.

Just like our children, we get angry sometimes and that is an emotional reality of life.

◊

I will have the courage to reveal my anger.

_____

_____

_____

_____

_____

November 20

FAMILY

*No matter what, I'll always have a big family around me...
my family ain't going to forget me and I ain't going to forget them.*
Willie Nelson

◊

When our children move away, we do not forget them, nor do they forget us. The spirit of family transcends miles. Family members continue to understand, support, and champion one another.

Our children may discount their family ties. Understanding what the family has done for them can take our children years. When the going gets tough our children find comfort in family. Having a family support system makes children and parents feel doubly loved.

◊

I will derive comfort from my family.

_____

_____

_____

_____

_____

November 21

FRIENDSHIP

Some of my best friends are children.

Ogden Nash

◊

Parent-child friendships are a controversial subject. Some of us are convinced that making friends with our children undermines parental authority. Others are convinced making friends with our children is a way of uniting generations.

The real issue here is friendship. When we are friends with someone, we are honest with them. Open. Ourselves. Surely parents and children can benefit from this kind of relationship. Being friends with our children is one of life's blessings.

◊

I will make friends with my children.

_____

_____

_____

_____

_____

November 22

WEARINESS

Sometimes when I lie down to sleep, I am overcome by weariness at the thought of what's ahead of me.

Eric Hoffer

◊

We want our children to have picture-perfect lives. The pursuit of perfection makes us worry about the next day, next week, next year. Some of us become chronic worriers.

After a restless night we awaken fatigued and more worried. Our worry accomplishes nothing. Why do we do this to ourselves? We can refuse to let worry rob us of life. Taking parenting one day at a time is a way of handling weariness and worry.

◊

I will take parenting one day at a time.

_____

_____

_____

_____

_____

November 23

THANKFULNESS

I want to thank you, Lord, for life and all that's in it.
                                                    Maya Angelou

◊

During this month of Thanksgiving we can be thankful for our children.

With the birth of a child, two separate personalities, one mother and one father, became a family. We may not always approve of our children's behavior, or the decisions they make, but we can still be thankful for them. Our lives are richer and truer because we are parents.

Today is the perfect day to give our kids extra hugs and say, "Thank you for being you."

◊

I will give thanks for my children.

_____

_____

_____

_____

_____

November 24

TEACHERS

The more parents can understand and support what teachers do, the more they can help their children.

Raymond Wlodkowski and Judith Jaynes

◊

Learning changes our children's lives.

Some of us have trouble understanding what our children's teachers are doing...let alone supporting their efforts. We can find viable alternatives, such as phone conferences, written reports, homework hot–lines, and access to lesson plans.

Teachers do their best when they know parents are supportive of their efforts.

◊

I will support my children's teachers whenever possible.

_____

_____

_____

_____

_____

November 25

QUESTIONS

Real conversation includes asking questions, and asking the right questions before it is too late.

Charles Schulz

◊

We grumble about not knowing our children. One way to get to know them is to ask questions. Questions show our children that we care about them, and help them to develop logical thought processes.

Some of the questions we ask our kids are painful. For them and for us. Because we love our children, we will ask the questions and listen attentively to the answers. "Why didn't I look into this sooner?" is a question we never want to ask. Or answer.

◊

I will ask questions before it is too late.

_____

_____

_____

_____

_____

November 26

DAYCARE

There is <u>no</u> contradiction between being a good mother
and leaving a child in the care of another adult for part of each day.
Sirgay Sanger, M.D. and John Kelly
◊

Dropping kids off at a daycare center makes many
parents cry inside. Mothers are especially vulnerable to
tears. In the recesses of our minds we believe good
mothers are supposed to stay at home.

But today's mothers are making history in finding
creative ways to pursue careers and parenting. We job–
share, work part–time and flex–time, freelance and start
home–based businesses. More importantly, we research
our daycare options and match the type of care to our
children's needs.

Let us feel confident enough about our parenting
to leave our children with competent caregivers. Our
children have fun with us *and* without us.
◊

I will have the confidence to leave my children with
competent caregivers.

_____

_____

_____

_____

_____

November 27

JOY

Pure joy is like bursting light; it explodes and swells within us.

Martha Cleveland

◊

Unless we have felt the darkest grief, we cannot appreciate the brightest joy.

The parents of run–away kids, chemically dependent kids, critically ill kids and terminally ill kids have grieved. None of us can second–guess life, however. Our situations could turn around in an instant. According to an ancient Chinese proverb, one joy has the power to scatter a hundred griefs.

Eventually joy will come to us, and when it does, we can share it with others. Joy changes lives.

◊

I will share my joy with others.

_____

_____

_____

_____

_____

November 28

GRANDPARENTS

The closest friends I have made through life have been people who also grew up close to a loved and loving grandmother or grandfather.

Margaret Mead

◊

Grandparents nurture our children in ways we cannot. Because grandparents have the wisdom that comes with age, they are more tolerant of our children's behavior.

Loving grandparents have a long-term affect on our children's lives. Our kids may recall the gifts their grandmother made for them or the shaggy dog stories their grandfather told. Later our children realize these casual acts were fraught with meaning.

◊

I will help my children get to know their grandparents.

_____

_____

_____

_____

_____

November 29

NUTRITION

We are allowing a majority of our children to form atrocious dietary habits.

Dr. Benjamin Spock

◊

Contrary to our children's opinions, salt, sugar and fat are not major food groups.

Researchers continue to study the affects of diet upon child development. Some researchers believe young children can be conditioned to certain foods. It is hard to buck food fads, but buck them we must, if we are to keep our children from developing atrocious eating habits.

We would be wise to monitor our children's eating. While we are at it, we can monitor our own.

◊

I will monitor my children's eating.

_____

_____

_____

_____

_____

November 30

VALUES

They (values) must be taught in the home, religious training, in the Boy Scouts and Girl Scouts, in little league and the media. And most critically, as a guarantee that everyone will be exposed to them, they must be taught in school.

James Michener

◊

Our children need values to live by. So we need to make our values clear and stand up for them.

We also need to connect our kids with community groups that teach values. First and foremost, our children need to know right from wrong. This concept may be reinforced in the classroom and at home. Some day our children will find emotional security in values. When everything else is gone, our children's values will remain.

Values keep kids going.

◊

I will instill good values in my children.

_____

_____

_____

_____

_____

December 1

FAMILY

We are the carriers of the spirit . . .

Allen Wheelis

◊

Family members tend to look alike. And, family members tend to think alike—they are carriers of the spirit.

Some families are known for their humor and others for their tenacity. The family values are passed from one generation to the next. Our children absorb these values and have a sense of belonging. As the family members scatter, however, our contacts often wane.

We help to hold the family together with family dinners, phone calls and letters. For as long as we live, we are carriers of the spirit.

◊

I will take steps to hold our family together.

_____

_____

_____

_____

_____

December 2

NEEDS

Taking care of your own needs is no easy task when you feel responsible for the needs of your family.

Harold Bloomfield, M.D. and Leonard Felder, Ph.D.

◊

Saying we put our children first sounds noble and good. In reality, we must put ourselves first.

Taking care of ourselves is the only way we will be able to take care of our children. Everyone is harmed by our self-neglect. Moaning about responsibilities makes our children feel guilty. When our children notice our self-neglect they feel even guiltier. Who needs guilt?

We are parents, and as such, can be mature enough to take good care of ourselves.

◊

I will take good care of myself.

_____

_____

_____

_____

_____

December 3

BUSYNESS

Why, there's hardly enough of me left to make <u>one</u> respectable person!

Lewis Carroll

◊

Holiday shopping is like a steeplechase race. We have no idea how we will place but we are determined to keep on running.

Busyness gets out of control and assumes a life of its own. Every day we feel more tense. There is not enough of us left to make one respectable person, let alone one responsible parent. Perhaps the most thoughtful gift we can give our children is the gift of calmness.

In calmness we find the joy of the season.

◊

I will balance holiday busyness with calmness.

_____

_____

_____

_____

_____

December 4

FATHERS

Fathering is, quite possibly, what I do most naturally and best. It is certainly what I most love.

Peter Jennings

◊

Being a sensitive father does not diminish masculinity. The "toughest" dads can have the daintiest of daughters. These fathers discover their newfound sensitivity applies to other areas of life.

Some dads take to fathering immediately and feel confident about it. The dads who are less secure feel lost for a while and ease into their roles. This is okay with kids. Our children do not want perfect fathers, they want fathers who love them. We can do that.

◊

I will be a loving father to my children.

_____

_____

_____

_____

_____

December 5

PEER PRESSURE

Isn't it a wonder how kids are so anxious to be grown up?
Bob Hope

◊

Our kids want to grow up fast. Daughters tell stories about everyone wearing make-up and sons want exclusive use of the family car.

These high pressure tactics are a reflection of the peer pressure our children feel. As badly as we feel about peer pressure, we cannot allow that pressure to pressure us. We can empathize with our children and assure them that privileges come with age.

Childhood is the prerequisite for adulthood. Our kids will be grown up before they know it.

◊

I will resist the pressure to force my children into early adulthood.

_____

_____

_____

_____

_____

December 6

FEELINGS

We need not walk on eggshells with our children for fear of leaving them with lingering guilt, and we should not hide our emotions when our kids disappoint us.

Alan Loy McGinnis

◊

Because we are afraid of our children's reactions, many of us stuff our feelings. We do not tell our children when we are disappointed in them.

Stuffing feelings is unfair to our children. Certainly, they will encounter honest feelings and spontaneous reactions in public. Our feedback may be just the nudge our children need to modify their behaviors.

We trust our children enough—and love them enough—to be truthful with our feelings.

◊

I will avoid walking on eggshells around my children.

_____

_____

_____

_____

_____

December 7

SELF-CONFIDENCE

Nothing promotes self-confidence more than the knowledge that you are a survivor.

Carole Gottleib and Carole Huatt

◊

Each of us has a different definition of survival. This is logical, since we have had varying experiences to survive. Although our experiences differ, one thing remains the same: The parents who survive are stronger for it.

After we have faced crisis and come to grips with it, our self-confidence grows. In turn, this self-confidence affects our children. Young children feel more secure, whereas older children pick up on coping methods. No matter how old our children are, they know they have self-confident parents.

◊

I will gain self-confidence from survival.

_____

_____

_____

_____

_____

December 8

LETTING GO

If try as you may you still do not know what to do, it is indeed best to do nothing.

Hugh Prather

◊

Do nothing? It sounds like a cop-out. What appears to be inaction can be a sign of intuitive parenting. We cannot fix everything for our children. Rather, we must let go of our children so they become independent.

Watching our children make the same mistakes, over and over again, is painful. Doing nothing is a test of our courage. We must have this kind of courage if our kids are going to figure out things for themselves. Letting go is critical to good parenting.

◊

I will have the courage to do nothing.

_____

_____

_____

_____

_____

December 9

SUPPORT

Good parenting is so subjective that it defies definition.
                    Robert Plutznig and Maria Laghi
                              ◊

Measuring our parenting success is difficult, if not impossible. Only when our children are well into adulthood do we get an indication of our success.

All through childhood we give our children positive strokes. Yet many of us are casual about doing the same for ourselves. Parents need positive strokes just as much as children. It is important for us to support other parents. Hug a parent today!
                              ◊

I will be supportive of other parents.

_____

_____

_____

_____

_____

December 10

LOVE

There's really no secret to working with kids. It all comes down to two things, loving them, and letting them know it.

Willard Scott

◊

Are you so preoccupied, you forget to tell your children that you love them? Unless we do this, and do it often, our children will never know the depth of our love. We can demonstrate love with hugs and smiles and laughter. We can verbalize our love in a short sentence or two. Whether we say it, shout it, sing it, write it or sign it, our kids will get the message. We LOVE them.

◊

I will tell my children I love them.

_____

_____

_____

_____

_____

December 11

INTELLIGENCE

You have the unique opportunity to boost your child's intelligence when it is most subject to change . . .

Joan Beck

◊

The early years of life are critical to the development of our children's intelligence. This means we must provide our children with good care **and** good experiences.

Babies respond to colorful mobiles and preschoolers benefit from short field trips. Creative experiences also foster the development of intelligence. Each day we have unique opportunities to boost our children's intelligence.

But we will do this lovingly, with an awareness of our children's individual personalities and needs.

◊

I will boost my children's intelligence in loving ways.

_____

_____

_____

_____

_____

December 12

HEALTH

Separate the deed from the doer.
                    Dr. Rudolf Dreikurs and Pearl Cassel
                                    ◊

Illness can make our children do strange things. Depressed children may develop irrational phobias and chemically dependent children may attempt suicide. Shocked parents do not know what to do next.

One thing we can do is separate the deed from the doer. We can mentally erase the affects of illness and focus upon the children we know. This exercise leads us to new modes of treatment for our children and serenity for ourselves.

                                    ◊

I will separate my children's deeds from the doers.

_____

_____

_____

_____

_____

December 13

MISTAKES

The nice thing is that now I know I can make a mistake or two before I'm through with this world, and it won't mean I'm unfit to live.

Betty Ford

◊

Hard as we try, some of us cannot forgive ourselves for our parenting mistakes. This behavior can frighten children, who know they are going to make lots of "boo-boos." Our children worry when the next slip will occur.

Making mistakes does not mean we are unfit parents, it means we are human parents. Forgiving ourselves is a way of assuring our children that we will forgive them. We can accept our parenting mistakes and move forward with life.

◊

I will accept my parenting mistakes.

_____

_____

_____

_____

_____

December 14

REALITY

By *helping a child to see reality as it is . . . we can instill in them the hope that it is within their power to change.*

Arnold Hutschnecker, M.D.

◊

Life is complicated enough without complicating reality. We are responsible for our children and that is the reality of our lives. Our children are responsible for their behavior and that is the reality of their lives.

Not only do we help our children to see reality, we can help them to face it. Only in facing reality will our children be able to cope with it. The realities of life are more exciting than fiction. Parents and children face reality together.

◊

I will help my children to face reality.

_____

_____

_____

_____

_____

December 15

COURTESY

The Everest of my ambition is to teach my children the simple precepts of existence.

Jean Kerr

◊

This quote may lead you to the question: What are the precepts of existence? Most of us think our children's existence should include personal hygiene, basic tidiness, and respectful behavior.

Alone, none of these qualities look formidable. Together these qualities can look like Mt. Everest. We wonder how we are going to get our children to cooperate. If we ask for help courteously, our children will be more apt to help. Courtesy counts.

◊

I will treat my children courteously.

_____

_____

_____

_____

_____

December 16

GOODNESS

And this our life exempt from public haunt
Finds tongues in trees, books in running brooks,
Sermons in stones, and good in everything.
                                        William Shakespeare

◊

Beauty is in the eye of the beholder, according to an old axiom. Goodness is also in the eye of the beholder. And we are beholders of our children.

Expecting goodness from our children elicits goodness from them. The wonderful thing about goodness is that it spreads from person to person, family to family and group to group. We see goodness everywhere, in soggy snowsuits, lost mittens, discarded boots, puddled floors and tired, rosy–cheeked children.

The goodness in our children is a living sermon—something to believe in and cherish.

◊

I will look for goodness in my children.

_____

_____

_____

_____

_____

December 17

BELIEFS

Believe in a child for what he is.

                                    Dorothy K. Whyte

◊

Signs of our children's talents appear in infancy. We watch for other signs to appear and wonder what vocations our children will choose.

Our children surprise us by going off in totally different directions. Observing our children's non-starts, jerky starts, and false starts drives us nuts. Parental advice falls on deaf ears. We can talk to our children about their talents, but what they do with their talents is their business.

We can encourage our children's talents without controlling their lives.

◊

I will encourage my children to develop their talents.

_____

_____

_____

_____

_____

December 18

JOY

Just the other morning I caught myself looking at my children for the pure pleasure of it.

Phyllis Theroux

◊

Everyone likes to watch children, including other people's children. Why? We are excited by children's energy.

Because we have too much to do; however, many of us don't really see our children. Lost in our own thoughts, we feed them, talk to them, clean for them and transport them. But looking closely at our children gives us clues about their general health, feelings and fantasies.

Looking at our children is one of life's greatest joys.

◊

I will look at my children and feel joy.

_____

_____

_____

_____

_____

December 19

CREATIVITY

Though the Earth rock and swell, yea, and though there be Wars and rumors of Wars, yet when Children draw, Dots and Circles will always be in the Ascendancy.

                                        Alice Lee Humphreys

◊

My first grader jumped off the school bus, dragging a painting behind her. The picture, round flowers spilling from an orange pot, was stunning in its simplicity. We decided to have the painting framed as a gift for her dad.

But the framer spoke patronizingly to my daughter and rushed us. We took our time anyway, choosing a mat and frame to enhance the painting. Evidently the framer was impressed. When we picked up the painting he unwrapped it carefully and praised my daughter's work.

Today, my daughter is a computer graphicist and artist. Her creativeness began early in life, with dots and circles and round flowers.

◊

I will remember that my children's creativity starts with scribbles.

December 20

WORRY

Small children disturb your sleep, big children your life.
                                        Yiddish Proverb

◊

We lie awake for hours, worrying about our kids and the temptations they face. Will they make the right choices?

Worrying makes us more upset and does nothing for our children. If our kids are not worried about a situation, what good does our worrying do? We cannot worry for our children, we can only guide them. In time, our children should assume responsibility for their own lives.

Let us temper our worries with faith. Our children can worry for themselves.

◊

I will temper my worries with faith.

_____

_____

_____

_____

_____

December 21

PLAY

As we play with our children, we are of course likely to grow closer to them.

Fred Rogers and Barry Head

◊

Playing with our children draws us closer to them. Many of us are good about playing with our children while they are young, but slack off as they get older.

A lot of thought goes into play. That is why we need to play with our adolescent and adult children. Our play takes different forms, camping, fishing, sailing, bowling, but it is play, nevertheless. There is nothing more joyous than playing with our children.

◊

I will play with my children today.

_____

_____

_____

_____

_____

December 22

SPIRITUALITY

When you unlatch the right door, your own special song will emerge loud and clear—and you'll be on your way to finding your life's meaning.

Rabbi Pesach Krauss and Morrie Goldfischer

◊

"It was bound to happen," we comment. "What a stroke of luck!" we exclaim. Both sentences sound like casual asides, but may actually be indicators of our Higher Power at work.

Step Two of the Twelve Steps talks about believing in a Power greater than ourselves. This belief can restore us to sanity and make us aware of the importance of spirituality. We are better parents if we take care of our physical and spiritual selves.

◊

I will nurture my spirituality.

_____

_____

_____

_____

_____

December 23

ENABLING

Would I could be by your side if you fall—
Would that my own heart could suffer all!

Edwin Markham

◊

No parent wants to see their child suffer. Some of us choose to suffer for our children, shielding them from decision making and the consequences of their decisions. Therapists call this behavior enabling.

We are enabling our children to remain dependent and immature. Would that our hearts could suffer all, but we must let our children work out their own problems. Our children do not learn from our experiences, they learn from their own.

◊

I will let my children learn from their own experiences.

_____

_____

_____

_____

_____

December 24

TIME

Time always seems long to the child who is waiting—for Christmas, for next summer, for becoming grown-up.

                                        Dag Hammarskjold

◊

Waiting is difficult for everyone, but it is most difficult for children. The children who are waiting for special holidays think time moves slowly. We are just the opposite and think time moves quickly.

The days we spend with our children are finite, precious units of time that will never come again. Each day of childhood is to be cherished. All too soon, our children will be grown, and we will be glad of the time we spent with them.

◊

I will cherish this day in time.

_____

_____

_____

_____

_____

December 25

MEMORIES

Through a child, I have been treated to Christmas.
                                        Robert Fulghum

◊

Our first daughter was born on Thanksgiving. When Christmas arrived she was 31 days old. How wonderful to have a baby in the house!

Because we were short of money, we bought a stubby tree and decorated it with the cheapest ornaments we could find. We placed our few gifts, bibs and rattles for the baby, beneath the tree. I was so excited about Christmas I was awake most of the night. My husband was just as excited and could hardly wait for morning.

Naturally, our baby was unaware of the significance of her first Christmas. As meager as our Christmas was, it was rich in love. Scenes from that time shine in my memory. Through a child, I am always treated to Christmas.

◊

I will derive happiness from parenting memories.

_____

_____

_____

_____

_____

December 26

GIVING

There is nothing more frustrating than buying a young-ster something she desperately wants, only to find she has become totally bored with it a few days later.

Michael Schulman and Eva Mekler

◊

Giving to our children usually gives us warm fuzzies. But sometimes giving backfires. We anticipate our children's joy in opening gifts, only to find their interest has evaporated. They want the latest products hyped on television.

We become angry at our children and ourselves. This might be a good time to back off. Happiness comes from giving thoughtful gifts to the children we love.

◊

I will feel happiness in giving.

_____

_____

_____

_____

_____

December 27

GOALS

I still want to change the world.

Ethel Kennedy

◊

Dedicated parents can have grandiose ideas. Our casual support grows into a fervent desire to change the world. We find ourselves going in all directions.

Instead of changing the entire world, we can change our corner of it. A small change can have a large impact upon the lives of children. With measured deliberation, we work to improve our children's lives.

One step at a time, one day at a time, our parenting goals will be achieved.

◊

I will work toward my goals one day at a time.

_____

_____

_____

_____

_____

December 28

SELF-WORTH

Learning to live with oneself, and enjoying this inner companion, is the first step toward living with children.

Eda Le Shan

◊

The parenting treadmill can make us feel guilty. We feel guilty about sitting down to read a magazine or asking the kids to be quiet during a television special.

The ability to enjoy our own company is critical to parenting. Once we are able to enjoy the inner companion within us, we are better able to enjoy our children. And our children find us more interesting.

When we are alone in the house we are not totally alone. We are in good company—ourselves.

◊

I will enjoy the companionship of self.

_____

_____

_____

_____

_____

December 29

SATISFACTION

Only when you put yourself first and follow your heart—changes that must come from within, can you find the satisfaction you've been missing.

Sonya Friedman, Ph.D.

◊

Parents would like to be guaranteed satisfaction. Better yet, we would like guarantees with money-back clauses. How do we find satisfaction?

We stop looking for it. The answers to our parenting questions are inside us. Meditation helps us to know ourselves, confront ourselves, and find the courage to change. In other words, we trust our feelings and go with them.

Parenting satisfaction does not come from our children, it comes from us.

◊

I will look for satisfaction inside myself.

_____

_____

_____

_____

_____

December 30

OBSOLESCENCE

The successful parent is one who does himself out of a job.
James and Mary Kenney

◊

Our children will leave us. Instead of mourning, we can choose to rejoice. The kids are right on schedule.

Through every age and stage of childhood our children are earning their independence. We are earning our independence, also. New pathways will be revealed to us in time. Until we find these pathways, we must remain open to life.

Successful parents anticipate doing themselves out of a job. Onward to new jobs and challenges!

◊

I will derive pleasure from doing myself out of a job.

December 31

CALMNESS

With calmness and humility I look forward to the future.
Albert Schweitzer

◊

How can we be calm when the world is in turmoil? How can we be calm when our lives are in turmoil?

We must not let the pace and confusion of modern life intrude upon our inner peace. Calmness dwells with us. No matter what happens, there are choices we can make. Quiet over noise. Hope over despair. Faith over doubt. With calmness at the core of our being we can face everything.

It is exciting to be alive. Because we love our children we continue to probe, reach, stretch, risk and dream. Tomorrow is waiting.

◊

I will anticipate the future calmly.

_____

_____

_____

_____

_____

BIBLIOGRAPHY

Albert, Linda and Popkin, Michael. *Quality Parenting*. New York: Random House, 1987, pp. 8, 17, 26, 40.

Anderson, Christopher. "Jaclyn Smith: I'm Still the Marrying Kind," *Journal*, August 1989, p. 62.

Andrews, Robert. *The Concise Columbia Dictionary of Quotations*. New York: Columbia University Press, 1989, pp. 188 and 189.

Angelou, Maya. *Poems*. New York: Bantam Books, 1986, p. 166.

Associated Press Wire Service. "Winning Them Over," *Star Tribune*, June 2, 1990, p. 1.

Avery, Caryl S. "Jackie: A Mother's Journey," *Journal*, March 1989, p. 198.

Bailey, Pearl. *Talking To Myself*. New York: Harcourt Brace Jovanovich, Inc., 1971, pp. 86, 118, 127.

Barr, Roseanne. *My Life As A Woman*. New York: Harper & Row, Publishers, 1989, pp. 201, 202.

Beck, Emily Morison, ed. *Bartlett's Familiar Quotations*. Boston: Little, Brown and Company, 1980, p. 681.

Beck, Joan. *How To Raise A Brighter Child*. New York: Pocket Books, 1986, pp. 2, 201, 204.

Berends, Polly Berrien. *Whole Child, Whole Parent*. New York: Harper & Row, Publishers, 1983, pp. 110, 250.

Berg, Elizabeth. "Gifts From Children," *Parents*, November 1989, p. 133.

Bettleheim, Bruno. *A Good Enough Parent*. New York: Alfred A. Knopf, 1987, pp. 13, 14, 171.

Bloom, Lynn Z. *Doctor Spock: Biography of A Conservative Radical*. Indianapolis: The Bobbs-Merrill Company, Inc., 1972, pp. 89, 90.

Bloomfield, Harold H. and Felder, Leonard, . *Making Peace With Yourself*. New York: Ballantine Books, 1985, pp. 53, 132, 141, 153.

Bodett, Tom. *As Far As You Can Go Without A Passport*. Reading: Addison-Wesley Publishing Company, Inc., 1985, pp. 53, 61, 80.

Bombeck, Erma. *If Life Is A Bowl Of Cherries—What Am I Doing In the Pits?* New York: Harcourt Brace Jovanovich, Inc., 1981, pp. 11,41.

Bracken, Peg. *A Window Over The Sink: A Mainly Affectionate Memoir*. New York: Harcourt Brace Jovanovich, Inc., 1981, pp. 96, 193.

Brazelton, T. Berry. *Doctor And Child*. Delacorte Press, 1976, pp. 100, 226.

Buchwald, Art. *You Can Fool All Of the People All Of The Time*. New York: Fawcett Columbine, 1985, p. 91.

Buck, Pearl S. *A Biography*. New York: The John Day Company, 1962, pp. 277, 283, 287.

Burns, George. *Gracie: A Love Story*. New York: G.P. Putnam's Sons, 1988, p. 126.

Buscaglia, Leo F. *Loving Each Other: The Challenge of Human Relationships*. New York: Fawcett Columbine, 1984, pp. 150, 189.

Buscaglia, Leo F. *Personhood*. New York: Ballantine Books, 1978, p. 126.

Carter, Hodding. "Mother and Child," *Good Housekeeping*, October 1990, p. 82.

Carter, Rosalynn. *First Lady From Plains*. Boston: Houghton Mifflin Company, 1984, pp. 66, 293.

Chapman, A.H. *Put-Offs And Come-Ons*. New York: G.P. Putnam's Sons, 1968, p. 27.

Chesler, Phyllis. *With Child: A Diary Of Motherhood*. New York: Thomas Y. Crowell, Publishers, 1979, pp. 183, 241.

Clemens, Samuel. *The Autobiography of Mark Twain*. New York: Harper & Brothers, Publishers, 1959, pp. 185, 213.

Cleveland, Martha. *Living Well: A Twelve-Step Response To Chronic Illness and Disability*. San Francisco: Harper/Hazelden, 1989, p. 89.

Conklin, Robert. *How To Get People To Do Things*. Chicago: Contemporary Books, Inc., 1979, p. 2, 21, 75.

Cosby, Bill. *Fatherhood*. New York: Berkley Books, 1987, Dedication.

Cosby, Bill. *Time Flies*. New York: Bantam Books, 1987, p. 117.

Cuomo, Mario. *Diaries of Mario M. Cuomo: The Campaign for Governor*. New York: Random House, 1984, p. 31, 114.

DeGrave, Louise. *From This Day Forward*. Boston: Little, Brown and Company, 1981, pp. 125, 127, 133.

DeMille, Cecil B. *The Autobiography of Cecil B. DeMille*. Englewood Cliffs: Prentice-Hall, Inc. 1959, p. 420.

DeSaint-Exupery. *The Little Prince*. New York: Harcourt, Brace and Company, 1943, Dedication and pp. 39, 70.

Day, Donald, ed. *The Autobiography of Will Rogers*. Boston: Houghton Mifflin Company, 1949, pp. 95, 385.

Dewey, John. *Experience and Education*. New York: The Macmillan Company, 1959, pp. 51, 55.

Donahue, Phil & Co. *Donohue: My Own Story*. New York: Simon and Schuster, 1979, pp. 7, 107, 110.

Dreikurs, Dr. Rudolf and Cassel, Pearl. *Discipline Without Tears*. New York: Hawthorn Books, 1972, pp. 49, 51.

Durwood, Peter. *Beatrix Potter: Creator of Peter Rabbit.* New York: The Kipling Press, 1988, p. 5.

Dyer, Wayne W. *What Do You Really Want For Your Children?* New York: William Morrow and Company, Inc. 1985, pp. 240, 241.

Ebert, Alan. "How 'Stanley Stunning' Became Peter Jennings," *Good Housekeeping*, April 1991, p. 50.

Elkind, David. *The Hurried Child: Growing Up Too Fast, Too Soon.* Reading: Addison-Wesley Publishing Company, 1981, pp. 192, 199.

Ellerbee, Linda. *Move On: Adventures in the Real World.* New York: G.P. Putnam's Sons, 1991, p. 266.

Ellman, Richard, comp/ed. *The New Oxford Book of American Verse.* New York: Oxford University Press, 1976, p. 259.

Ellsworth, Barry A. *Living In Love With Yourself.* Salt Lake City: Breakthrough Publishing, 1988, pp. 9, 41, 156.

Feinberg, Mortimer R., Feinberg, Gloria and Tarrant, John J. *Leavetaking: When and How to Say Goodbye.* New York: Simon and Schuster, 1978, pp. 42, 257, 262.

Felder, Leonard. *A Fresh Start.* New York: New American Library, 1987, p. 114.

Ferrel, Robert H., Editor. *Off The Record: The Private Papers of Harry S. Truman.* New York: Harper & Row, Publishers, 1980, p. 124.

Finston, Peggy. *Parenting Plus: Raising Children With Special Needs.* New York: Dutton, 1990, pp. 68, 77, 79.

Ford, Betty. *Betty: A Glad Awakening.* Garden City: Doubleday & Company, Inc. 1987, pp. 205, 207.

Frank, Joseph and Goldestein, David I. *Selected Letters of Fyodor Dostoyevsky.* New Brunswick: Rutgers University Press, 1987, pp. 280, 286.

Franklin, Benjamin. *Poor Richard's Almanack.* Mount Vernon: Peter Pauper Press.

Friedman, Jack and Shaw, Bill. "The Quiet Victories of Ryan White," *People*, May 30, 1988, p. 88.

Friedman, Sonya. "Isn't It Time To Please Yourself?" *Journal*, February 1991, pp. 89, 154.

Fromm, Erich. *On Disobedience and Other Essays.* New York: The Seabury Press, 1981, p.3.

Fulghum, Robert. *All I Really Need To Know I Learned In Kindergarten.* New York: Villard Books, 1990, pp. 78, 93, 136.

Gaylin, Willard. *Caring.* New York: Alfred A. Knopf, 1976, pp. 149, 173, 179.

George, David L., ed. *The Family Book of Best Loved Poems.* Garden City: Doubleday & Company, Inc., 1952, pp. 76, 154, 183, 190, 261, 285.

Gibran, Kahlil. *The Prophet.* New York: Alfred A. Knopf, 1976, p. 17.

Ginott, Hiam. *Between Parent and Child.* New York: The Macmillan Co., 1967, p. 33

Goodman, Ellen. *Making Sense.* New York: The Atlantic Monthly Press, 1989, pp. 290, 299, 359.

Greene, Bob. *Good Morning Merry Sunshine: A Father's Journal of His Child's First Year.* New York: Antheneum, 1984, pp. 171, 255.

Groller, Ingrid. "Jon Voight: A Father's Reflections," *Parents,* May 1983, p. 148.

Guth, Dorothy Lobrano, ed. *Letters of E.B. White.* New York: Harper & Row, Publishers, 1976, pp. 99, 103.

Hammarskjold, Dag. *Markings.* New York: Alfred A. Knopf, 1964, pp. 5, 93.

Hayes, Helen. *Loving Life: Promises and Problems, Pains and Joys.* Garden City: Doubleday & Company, Inc., 1987, p. 46.

Heller, Scott. "A Place In The Heart," *People,* October 17, 1988, p. 98.

Hibbert, Christopher. *Queen Victoria: In Her Letters And Journals.* New York: Viking Penquin Inc., 1985, p. 94.

Hoffer, Eric. *Before the Sabbath.* New York: Harper & Row, Publishers, 1979, p. 40.

Holliday, Robert Cortes. *Joyce Kilmer.* Garden City: Doubleday, Doran & Company, Inc. 1945, pp. 186, 217.

Holloway, Emory. *Walt Whitman: Complete Poetry & Selected Prose and Letters.* London: The Nonesuch Press, 1971, pp. 136, 935.

"Hollywood Moms," *McCall's,* October 1988, p. 44, 45. (Bette Midler and Mia Farrow quotes.)

Holm, Bill. *Prairie Days.* Dallas: Saybrook Publishing Co., 1987, pp. 2, 87.

Holmes, Oliver Wendell. *The Autocrat of the Breakfast Table.* Philadelphia: Henry Altemus, 1897, p. 214.

Holt, John. *Learning All The Time.* Reading: Addison-Wesley Publishing Company, Inc., 1989, pp. 130, 140.

Holt, Pat and Ketterman, Grace. *When You Feel Like Screaming! Help For Frustrated Mothers.* Wheaton: Harold Shaw, 1988, p. 59.

Holy Bible, King James version. London: Collins' Clear-Type Press, 1941, Proverbs 15:1, Proverbs 22:6.

Hooks, William H., ed. *The Pleasure of Their Company: How To Have More Fun With Your Children.* Radnor: Chilton Book Company, 1981, p. 2.

Hope, Bob. *Have Tux, Will Travel.* New York: Simon and Schuster, 1954, pp. 293, 295, 298.

Hostetler, John A., ed. *Amish Roots: A Treasury of History, Wisdom, And Lore.* Baltimore: The Johns Hopkins University Press, 1989, p. 112.

Humphreys, Alice Lee. *Angels In Pinafores.* Richmond: John Knox Press, 1971, pp. 12, 89.

Hutchins, Robert Marynard, ed. *Great Books of the Western World: The Plays and Sonnets of William Shakespeare*. New York: Encyclopedia Britannica, Inc., 1952, p. 603.

Hutschnecker, Arnold A. *Hope: The Dynamics of Self-Fulfillment*. New York: G.P. Putnam's Sons, 1981, p. 143.

Hyatt, Carole and Gottlieb, Linda. *When Smart People Fail*. New York: Simon and Schuster, 1987, pp. 35, 236.

Jerome, Jim. "24-Karat Goldie!", *People*, June 11, 1990, p. 84.

Johnston, Johanna and Karmiller, Murray, eds. *Family Tree*. Cleveland: The World Publishing Company, 1967, p. 493.

Joseph, Stephen M. *Children In Fear*. New York: Holt, Rinehart and Winston, 1974, p. 65.

Kagan, Jerome. *The Nature of the Child*. New York: Basic Books, Inc., Publishers, 1984, p. 269.

Kaplan, Leslie S. *Coping With Peer Pressure*. New York: The Rosen Publishing Group, Inc., 1987, p. 46.

Kaplan, Louise J. *Oneness and Separateness: From Infant to Individual*. New York: Simon and Schuster, 1978, p. 31.

Keillor, Garrison. *Happy To Be Here*. New York: Penquin Books, 1983, p. 253.

Kennedy, Eugene. *A Time For Being Human*. Chicago: The Thomas More Press, 1977, pp. 110, 148.

Kennedy, Rose Fitzgerald. *Times To Remember*. Garden City: Doubleday & Company, Inc., 1974, pp. 76, 85, 99.

Kenney, James and Kenney, Mary. *Whole-Life Parenting*. New York: Continuum, 1982, pp. 29, 218.

Kerr, Jean. *How I Got To Be Perfect*. Garden City: Doubleday & Co. Inc., 1978, p. 236.

Kerr, Jean. *Please Don't Eat The Daisies*. Garden City: Doubleday & Company, Inc., 1957, pp. 147, 150, 157.

King, Coretta Scott. *My Life With Martin Luther King, Jr*. New York: Rinehart and Winston, 1969, p. 107.

Kleinfield, Sonny. "Lee Iacocca: Straight Talk On His Kids, His Mother, His Divorce," *Good Housekeeping*, November 1988, p. 136.

Klobuchar, Jim. *When We Reach For the Sun*. Stillwater: Voyageur Press, 1987, pp. 8, 28, 64.

Kohl, Herbert. *Growing Up With Your Children*. Boston: Little, Brown and Company, 1978, pp. 314, 321, 322.

Krauss, Pesach and Goldfischer, Morrie. *Why Me? Coping With Grief, Loss, and Change*. New York: Bantam Books, 1990, pp. 62, 153.

Kushner, Harold. *Who Needs God*. New York: Pocket Books, 1989, pp. 10, 34, 172.

LeShan, Eda L. *How To Survive Parenthood*. New York: Random House, 1965, pp. 237, 238.

LeSourd, Leonard, ed. *Catherine Marshall: A Closer Walk*. Old Tappan, NJ: Chosen Books, 1986, pp. 116, 153.

Landers, Ann. *The Ann Landers Encyclopedia A to Z*. New York: Ballantine Books, 1978, pp. 832, 837.

Lathem, Edward Connery, ed. *The Poetry of Robert Frost*. New York: Holt, Rinehart and Winston, 1969, pp. 403, 225.

Leefeldt, Christine and Callenback, Ernest. *The Art of Friendship*. New York: Pantheon Books, 1979, p. 4.

Lerner, Harriet Goldhor. *The Dance Of Anger*. New York: Harper & Row, 1985, pp. 3, 9, 215.

Levenson, Sam. *You Don't Have To Be In Who's Who To Know What's What*. Boston: G.K. Hall & Co., 1980, pp. 44, 45, 46.

Lindberg, Anne Morrow. *Hour of Gold, Hour of Lead*. New York: Harcourt Brace Jovanovich, 1973, pp. 215, 219.

Lindberg, Charles A. *We*. New York: Grosset & Dunlap Publishers, 1927, p. 225.

Lowenfeld, Viktor. *Creative and Mental Growth*. New York: The Macmillan Company, 1956, pp. 11, 53.

McBride, Angela Barron. *The Growth and Development of Mothers*. New York: Harper & Row, Publishers, 1973, pp. xiii, 59, 150.

McGinley, Phyllis. *Times Three*. New York: Viking Press, 1961, p. 182.

McGinnis, Alan Loy. *Bringing Out The Best In People*. Minneapolis: Augsburg Publishing House, 1985, pp. 57, 124, 183, 127.

Markham, Edwin, ed. *The American Book of Poetry*. New York: William H. Wise & Co., 1938, p. 263.

Martignoni, Margaret E. *The Illustrated Treasury of Children's Literature*. New York: Grosset & Dunlap, Inc., 1955, pp. 297, 299.

Mastrich, Jim and Birnes, Bill. *Strong Enough For Two: How To Overcome Codependence and Other Enabling Behavior and Take Control of Your Life*. New York: Collier Books, 1990, p. 142.

Mayo, Charles. *Mayo: The Story of My Family and My Career*. Garden City: Doubleday & Company, 1968, pp. 311, 347.

Mead, Margaret. *Blackberry Winter*. New York: William Morrow & Company, 1972, p. 257.

Medeiros, Donald C. Porter, Barbara J., and Welch, I. David. *Children Under Stress: How To Help With the Everyday Stress of Childhood*. Englewood Cliffs, NJ: Prentice-Hall, Inc., 1983, pp. 45, 131.

Meir, Golda. *My Life*. New York: Dell Publishing Co., Inc., 1935, p. 93.

Merton, Thomas. *No Man Is An Island*. New York: Harcourt, Brace and Company, 1955, pp. 126, 127.

Michener, James A. "What is the Secret of Teaching Values?" *Life*, April 1991.

Miller, Mary Susan. *Bringing Learning Home*. New York: Harper & Row, Publishers, 1981, pp. 10, 99, 225.

Milne, A.A. *Autobiography*. New York: E.P. Dutton & Co., Inc., 1939, pp. 283, 287.

Murphy, Edward F. *2,715 One-Line Quotations for Speakers, Writers & Raconteurs*. New York: Bonanza Books, 1989, pp. 150, 185.

Murphy, Edward F. *The Crown Treasury of Relevant Quotations*. New York: Crown Publishers, Inc. 1978, p. 134.

Nash, Ogden. *Family Reunion*. Boston: Little, Brown and Company, 1950, p. 7.

Naylor, Phyllis. *In Small Doses*. New York: Antheneum, 1979, pp. 30, 39, 51, 160.

Nelson, Willie. *Willie: An Autobiography*. New York: Simon & Schuster Inc., Pocket Books, 1988, p. 310, 311.

Okimoto, Jean Davies and Stegall, Phyllis Jackson. *Boomerang Kids*. Boston: Little, Brown and Company, 1987, p. 64, 165.

Partnow, Elaine, ed. *The Quotable Woman*. Los Angeles: Pinnacle Books, Inc., 1977, p. 50.

"Passages," *People*, August 6, 1990, p. 99 (see Karl Menninger quote).

Pearce, Joseph Chilton. *Magical Child: Recovering Nature's Plan For Our Children*. New York: Bantam Books, 1986, p. 218.

Pearsall, Paul. *Super Joy: Learning To Celebrate Everyday Life*. New York: Doubleday, 1988, p. 58.

Peck, M. Scott. *The Road Less Traveled*. New York: Simon and Schuster, 1978, pp. 64, 253.

Pepper, Margaret. *The Harper Religious & Inspirational Quotation Companion*. New York: Harper & Row, Publishers, 1989, p. 76.

Piers, Maria W. and Landau, Genieve Millet. *The Gift of Play: And Why Young Children Cannot Thrive Without It*. New York: Walker and Company, 1980, p. 51, 53, 115.

Prather, Hugh. *Notes On How To Live In The World And Still Be Happy*. New York: Doubleday, 1986, pp. 1, 54, 78.

Prochnow, Herbert V. and Prochnow, Herbert V., Jr. *A Treasury of Humorous Quotations*. New York: Harper & Row, Publishers, 1969, pp. 54, 250.

Plutznik, Roberta and Laghi, Maria. *The Private Lives of Parents*. New York: Everest House Publishers, 1983, pp. 7, 237.

Petrucelli, Alan W. "Carol Burnett: 'Talk To Your Kids—I Finally Did,'" *Redbook*, February 1989.

Radcliffe, Donnie. *Simply Barbara Bush*. New York: Warner Books, 1989, p. 177.

Reicks, Rod. "Family Awareness Lets Benatar Take A Long View in Life," *Rochester Post-Bulletin*, November, 1988, p. 2-C.

Rinzer, Carol Eisen. *Your Adolescent: An Owner's Manual.* New York: Atheneum, 1981, p. 23.

Rivers, Caryl and Lupe, Alan. *For Better, For Worse.* New York: Summit Books, 1981, pp. 123, 147.

Rivers, Joan with Meryman, Richard. *Enter Talking.* New York: Delacorte Press, 1986, p. 106.

Robyns, Gwen. *Princess Grace: A Biography.* New York: David McCay Company Inc., 1976. pp. 201, 263, 266.

Rogers, Fred and Head, Barry. *Mister Rogers Playbook.* New York: Berkley Books, 1975, pp. 11, 15, 230.

Roosevelt, Eleanor. *The Biography of Eleanor Roosevelt.* New York: Harper & Brothers Publishers, 1961, p. 283.

Ruddick, Sara and Daniels, Pamela, eds. *Working It Out: 23 Women Writers, Artists, Scientists and Scholars Talk About Their Lives and Work.* New York: Pantheon Books, 1977, p. 36.

Sadat, Jehan. *A Woman of Egypt.* New York: Simon and Schuster, 1987, pp. 169, 171.

Salk, Lee. *Preparing for Parenthood.* New York: David McKay Company, Inc., 1974, p. 146.

Samalin, Nancy. *Loving Your Child Is Not Enough.* New York: Viking Penguin, Inc., 1987, pp. 31, 50, 131.

Sanger, Sirgay and Kelly, John. *The Woman Who Works, The Parent Who Cares.* San Francisco: Harper/Hazelden, 1988, p. 35.

Schindehette, Susan, Alexander, Michael, Carter, Alan and Podolsky, J.D. "Kermit, Miss Piggy, Big Bird, Grover and Kids All Over the World Mourn the Loss of Muppetmeister Jim Henson", *People*, May 28, 1990.

Schulman, Michael and Mekler, Eva. *Bringing Up A Moral Child.* New York: Addison-Wesley Publishing Group, 1985, pp. 164, 269.

Schulz, Charles. *You Don't Look 35 Charlie Brown!* New York: Holt, Rinehart and Winston, 1985.

Schwartz, Alvin, comp. *To Be A Father.* New York: Crown Publishers, 1967, pp. xviii, 43.

Schweitzer, Albert. *Out of My Life and Thought: An Autobiography.* New York: Henry Holt and Company, 1949, pp. 231, 242, 266.

Sciacca, Joe. "Ethel Kennedy," *Journal*, January 1991, p. 68.

Scott, Vernon. "Valerie Harper: Everything Is Coming Up 'Love'" *Good Housekeeping*, June 1990, p. 129.

Scott, Willard. *The Joy of Living.* New York: Ballantine Books, 1982, p. 95.

Sendak, Maurice. *Caldecott & Company: Notes On Books & Pictures*. New York: Farrar, Straus and Giroux, 1988, p. 207.

Shedd, Charlie. *You Can Be A Great Parent!* Waco: Word Books, 1978, p. 85.

Sherman, Eric. John Goodman: The Busiest Guy Around," *Journal*, January 1991, p. 68.

Sills, Beverly and Linderman, Laurence. *Beverly: An Autobiography*. New York: Bantam Books, 1987, p. 138.

Silverstein, Shel. *Where The Sidewalk Ends*. New York: Harper & Row, Publishers, Inc., 1974, p. 27.

Spock, Benjamin. *Dr. Spock On Parenting*. New York: Pocket Books, 1988, pp. 39, 335.

Strassfeld, Sharon and Green, Kathy. *The Jewish Family Book*. New York: Bantam Books, 1981, pp. 320, 378.

Swindoll, Charles R. *Living On the Ragged Edge: Coming To Terms With Reality*. New York: Bantam Books, 1988, p. 224.

Taraborrelli, J. Randy. *Laughing Till It Hurts: The Complete Life and Career Of Carol Burnett*. New York: William Morrow and Company, 1988, pp. 347, 369, 392.

Theroux, Phyllis. "Being There," *Parents*, October, 1987, p. 60.

Theroux, Phyllis. "The Parent As Audience," *Parents*, October 1985, p. 55.

Thomas, Bob. "Cosby Talks," *Good Housekeeping*, February, 1991, p. 217.

Ustinov, Peter. *Dear Me*. New York: Penguin Books, 1979, p. 337.

Viorst, Judith. *Necessary Losses*. New York: Ballantine Books, 1986, pp. 37, 256, 261.

Viscott, David. *Risking*. New York: Pocket Books, 1979, pp. 35, 63, 88.

Veniga, Robert. *A Gift of Hope*. Boston: Little, Brown and Company, 1985, p. 270.

Von Trapp, Maria. *Yesterday, Today and Forever*. Harrison: New Leaf Press, 1975, p. 9.

Walker, Ellen. *Growing Up With My Children: Reflections of a Less Than Perfect Parent*. Center City, MN: Hazelden Educational Materials, 1988, pp. 37, 38, 57.

Walters, Barbara. *How To Talk With Practically Anybody About Practically Anything*. Garden City: Doubleday & Company, Inc., 1970, p. 66.

Wheelis, Allen. *On Not Knowing How To Live*. New York: Harper & Row, Publishers, 1975, pp. 5, 17.

Whitman, Walt. *Leaves of Grass*. New York: Grosset & Dunlap, 1971, p. 175.

Whyte, Dorothy K. *Teaching Your Child Right From Wrong*. Boston: The Bobbs-Merrill Company, pp. 104, 180.

Willius, Frederick A.. *Aphorisms of Dr. Charles Horace Mayo and Dr. William James Mayo*. Rochester, MN Mayo Foundation for Medical Education and Research, 1988, p. 11.

Winn, Marie, ed. *The Fireside Book of Children's Songs*. New York: Simon and Schuster, 1966, p. 26.

Wlodkowski, Raymond and Jaynes, Judith H. *Eager to Learn*. San Francisco: Jossey-Bass Inc., Publishers, 1990, pp. xii, 17, 87.

Woods, K.W. "Hollywood's Most Romantic Love Matches—Stars in Their Eyes," *Journal*, February 1991, p. 24.

Wright, Frank Lloyd. *An Autobiography: Frank Lloyd Wright*. New York: Horizons Press, 1977, p. 134.

Yates, Susan Alexanter. *And Then I Had Kids: Encouragement for Mothers of Young Children*. Brentwood, TN: Wolgemuth & Hyatt Publishers, Inc. 1990, p. 193.

York, Phyllis & David and Wachtel, Ted. *Toughlove*. Garden City: Doubleday & Company, 1982, pp. 20, 103, 149.

Yutang, Lin, ed. *The Wisdom of Confucius*. New York: Random House, 1938, p. 247.

INDEX

Ability   January 29
Acceptance   February, 23, April 1, June 13, October 22
Actions   January 26
Adolescence   January 21, February 12, August 17,October 16, November 14
Adoption   June 21
Adult Children of
   Alcoholics   November 17
Aging   March 16, September 11
Aloneness   September 8
Ambivalence   January 12
Amusement   September 21
Anger   March 25, June 4, September 29, November 19
Approval   July 8
Arguing   June 15
Assessment   April 11
Attention   July 4
Attitude   March 4, May 27, June 14
Autonomy   June 7
Awareness   August 18, October 30
Balance   November 9
Beauty   April 6, October 31
Behavior   April 3, June 22, July 18, October 4
Beliefs   December 17, February 11
Birthdays   January 15
Blame   June 16
Busyness   December 3
Calmness   March 23, December 31
Caring Time   January 28
Change   January 1, March 17, June 11, August 7, September 9
Childcare   January 7, March 26, April 18, May 29, June 26, September 28
Child Development   August 27
Childhood   February 28, June 19, July 29, August 25
Choices   March 19
Chores   June 24, August 11
Common Sense   August 30
Communication   January 23, April 12, August 2, September 4
Competition   May 19
Complaining   June 3
Compulsion   February 29
Connectedness   March 15, June 17, October 28
Connections   February 18
Constancy   March 30
Consequences   September 30
Control   January 27, August 5, October 8
Conversation   February 21
Coping   April 4, August 19
Courage   April 14, June 25
Courtesy   December 15
Creativity   January 14, July 30, October 26, December 19
Criticism   October 4
Daycare   November 26
Demands   November 2
Dependence   January 25, February 4
Direction   October 13
Discipline   March 6, May 11, May 30, June 30, October 23,

	November 18
Dreams	January 9, September 25
Empathy	August 13
Empty-Nest	January 10, September 1, February 9
Enabling	December 23
Equality	March 11, October 19
Expectations	May 22
Experience	June 12, September 19
Expressions	January 18
Family	March 27, April 21, May 13, May 26, July 31, August 15, September 10, November 20, December 1
Fathers	August 20, December 4
Failure	March 29, October 10, November 7
Fatigue	November 22
Feelings	February 20, March 2, April 26, July 5, August 3, September 23, December 6
First–born	February 15
Forgiveness	February 16, June 10, August 31
Friendship	April 24, November 21
Genetics	May 28
Giving	February 14, May 4, December 26
Goals	May 5, December 27
Goodness	December 16
Grandparents	November 28
Gratitude	February 4
Grief	October 12
Growth	October 2
Guidance	November 4
Guilt	August 28
Happiness	January 30, February 8, March 5, March 9, April 25, May 17, May 27, July 17
Health	May 24, December 12
Helping	January 27
Heritage	January 6, January 8, January 31
Honesty	September 16, November 8
Hope	August 8, November 5
Housekeeping	October 20
Humor	June 28, September 13
Identity	January 8, May 2
Illness	January 17
Immediacy	January 4, January 29, March 8, April 2, August 22, September 5
Imperfection	January 5, February 18
Importance	July 21
Independence	April 30, June 5, July 20
Infants	July 23
Intelligence	May 23, December 11
Interests	July 5
Involvement	April 8
Joy	April 5, June 14, September 18, November 27, December 18
Kindness	April 28, October 6
Learning	February 3, March 3, April 13, September 2
Leave–taking	February 5
Letting Go	January 20, February 17, May 16, June 7, October 15, December 8
Limits	October 21
Listening	February 22
Loneliness	February 2
Love	January 1, January 16, May 20, June 9, July 15, August 12, August 24, November 16, December 10
Maturation	September 14

Maturity	March 1, July 6
Meal–time	February 7
Memories	April 22, July 2, October 17, December 25
Mental Health	November 12
Messiness	July 24
Minutiae	August 26
Mistakes	Decembr 13
Mothers	July 11, October 11, November 6
Naturalness	November 10
Needs	May 25, December 2
Nicknames	October 9
Nutrition	February 7, May 8, November 29
Nurturing	July 27
Obsolescense	December 3
Openness	May 15
Optimism	June 20
Pain	February 26, April 15, May 14
Partnership	July 13
Patience	January 2, April 19
Peacefulness	February 25
Peers	June 27
Peer Pressure	July 12, December 5
Perception	March 14, August 10, October 18
Perfection	July 28
Personality	March 22, April 7, April 10, June 23
Personhood	April 7
Perspective	April 16, August 10
Pets	June 18, September 7
Play	March 31, May 7, July 19, September 20, December 21
Positives	September 29
Possessions	September 15
Praise	April 18, July 10, October 29
Pride	January 13
Priorities	March 18, April 29, September 17
Problems	August 6, September 24
Progress	July 16
Promises	June 11
Quiet Time	March 7, May 9, October 24, November 13
Questions	November 25
Reality	July 22, September 12, December 14
Recreation	September 21
Relationships	February 10, August 4
Renewal	May 1
Respect	May 10, July 26
Responsibility	January 19, August 11, September 22
Risking	April 27
Roles	April 20, May 3
Role Models	January 3, February 6, September 3
Role Reversal	January 24
Rules	February 1
Satisfaction	December 29
Seasons	June 1, November 3
Security	February 24, August 1, August 23
Self-awareness	February 9
Self-care	January 17, April 17, June 29, July 7
Self-confidence	December 7
Self-concept	August 21
Self-discovery	March 13
Self-doubt	January 11
Self-esteem	October 25
Self-forgiveness	February 16
Self-help	July 14

Self-image	August 20, November 2
Self-love	January 22
Self-reliance	March 20
Self-worth	February 19, September 27, December 28
Serenity	February 27
Spirituality	February 13, June 8, July 3, December 22
Sports	May 24
Stability	June 6, July 3
Stories	November 1
Stress	March 24, May 12, May 21, August 16
Struggle	October 14
Support	September 6, October 1, December 9
Talent	April 23, June 2
Talk	August 29
Tantrums	July 9
Teachers	November 24
Thankfulness	November 23
Thinking	May 31
Thoughts	November 25, December 17
Time	February 8, March 21, May 18, October 7, December 24
Tolerance	August 9
Toughness	October 5
Toymaking	August 14
Tradition	March 10
Trends	November 15
Uniqueness	October 3
Values	March 12, April 2, September 26, November 30
Visualization	April 9
Weakness	November 11
Weariness	November 22
Workaholics	July 1
Wisdom	May 6, July 25
Wonder	January 7
Work	March 28
Worry	February 13, October 27, December 20